PUBLIC
RELATIONS
FOR
PUBLIC
LIBRARIES

PUBLIC RELATIONS FOR PUBLIC LIBRARIES

BETTY RICE

CREATIVE PROBLEM SOLVING

The H. W. Wilson Company   New York   1972

Library of Congress Cataloging in Publication Data
Rice, Betty.
    Public relations for public libraries.
    Bibliography: p.
    1.   Public relations — Libraries.   I.   Title.
Z716.3.R48   659.2′9′0274   72-2421
ISBN 0-8242-0476-X

CONTENTS

1

PUBLIC RELATIONS
IS A WAY OF LIFE

Public relations is a way of life. Any institution which hopes to achieve that degree of flexibility and responsiveness to public opinion which will ensure its survival finds public relations a necessity. Public relations involves a continuing appraisal of one's situation, one's attitudes, and one's progress toward well-defined goals.

Yet to many librarians the very words "public relations" have unpleasant commercial overtones. This professional disdain in some cases may stem from confusion in terminology and in others from a lack of historical perspective. It is probably more difficult to tell what public relations *is* than what it *is not*. To narrow our field, let us begin by examining public relations from a slightly negative standpoint.

Advertising is not public relations. Advertising is the purchasing of space in a periodical or of time on radio and television to express a viewpoint or to sell a product. Whether or not the viewpoint or the product is acceptable to the publisher of the magazine or the manager of the station has little relationship to the release of the message. The reader or the audience receives the message because its transmission has been paid for. Advertising is a commercial transaction through which the purchaser of space or time may reach his prospects with a message of his own devising, couched in language he has chosen and released at a time convenient to his purpose. Although certain types of advertising — those which feature the "good name" or reputation of the manufacturer rather than his product (known as "institutional advertising") may be supportive of a public relations program, advertising in its usual format is not public relations and can play only a tangential role in the total public relations program of any organization.

Publicity is not public relations. Publicity consists of the release of information to the public about an institution, a product, a person or an event through channels of communication (newspapers, magazines, radio, television) whose space or time has not been paid for. This makes publicity a far more delicate instrument than advertising. A newspaper unwilling to give free publicity to those it opposes may be perfectly willing to accept a paid political advertisement for an individual whose candidacy is being attacked in its own editorial columns.

Publicity is the handmaiden of public relations. When used as a legitimate method of placing information before the public, a well-written, properly-distributed publicity release performs a worthwhile service and there are very few newspaper editors who would deny that they welcome intelligently prepared material from trustworthy sources. The small weekly newspaper may use the material exactly as submitted. The medium-size daily may rewrite the item to conform to its own style or to play up a slightly different aspect of the story, thus minimizing the "canned" aspects of the material. The sophisticated metropolitan daily may even dispatch a reporter to ferret out a new angle for exclusive presentation to its readers. In each case, the impetus for publishing news about the institution, product, person or event came from the publicity release and the coverage received stemmed from the interest generated. Publicity must stand on its own merits. Advertising supports the paper; news releases can help to make it readable.

Publicity is not, however, press agentry, which is outmoded these days except as practiced in the entertainment field. When a story "leaks out" that a much-married motion picture star is going to receive for her birthday a mammoth pearl whose price in thousands of dollars corresponds to her age, that's press agentry. Personalities are merchandised with little regard for human values, and the old P. T. Barnum wheeze, "I don't care what you say about me as long as you mention my name," still holds good for many figures in the public eye. It is almost inconceivable that this type of hard-sell promotion would form part of a successful public relations program for any institution hoping to retain the public's confidence over a long period of time.

Public relations is not a child of the twentieth century although it has achieved respectability as a profession during this era. Some practitioners view the Egyptian pyramids as an early form of public relations — an awe-inspiring and continuing message about the divinity of royalty directed to a population largely unable to read. During the French and American revolutions, pamphleteers were busy trying to influence the thinking of the man in the street. According to George Washington, Thomas Paine's *Common Sense* so stirred the colonists that it "worked a powerful change in the minds of many men."

The Civil War saw further efforts to influence large groups of people on both sides of the Atlantic to active partisanship. Efforts to sell bonds during wartime, to keep morale high, to restore confidence in the economy during a depression, to maintain the prestige of a nation, to elect a President — all of these activities reflect some facet of the public relations processes although the average person may be unaware of this fact. While historically public relations efforts may have taken different forms, the *ultimate intent* is identical. The intent is to present a case for the merits of a cause or an institution so cogently, so winningly, so irresistibly that the hearts and minds of men will be captured and support the objectives set forth. Public relations is "the engineering of consent," to use the capsule definition of Edward L. Bernays, dean of practitioners in this field.

Genuine public relations is not "making it look good." If the basic product (in our case, the library in its totality) is a bad product, no amount of fancy packaging can disguise the shoddy contents over a prolonged period of time. Neither is public relations an esoteric practice understood only by a few initiates. Everyone understands good manners, patience, small kindnesses, a sympathetic attitude toward the unreasonableness of human beings — these qualities are fundamental to a good public relations program.

Public libraries belong in the ranks of those once unchallenged institutions, the schools, the universities, the churches, and constitutional government. During recent years, each of these once firmly founded institutions has experienced internal dissent and external attack. Whether public libraries, dependent upon public funds and therefore, by obvious extension, upon public goodwill for their very existence can avoid the maelstrom is a serious question. In the measure that public libraries are aware of and responsive to the needs, demands, and desires of the publics they should serve, it is possible that they will preserve their freedom of action, their much-prized objectivity, and their privilege of serving all segments of the community with intelligent impartiality.

To remove a few "Silence, please!" signs and hastily assemble a collection of paperbacks is not sufficient evidence that a library has assessed its situation, analyzed the publics it should serve, and blocked out a long-term program of action (with short-term benchmarks) to achieve a realistic relationship with past, present, and potential patrons. Such a total program is what the author classifies as genuine public relations.

How a library interprets its regulations to the public; whether or not there is a sincere attempt to anticipate the emerging needs of the community and to prepare in advance to meet them; how frequently accepted methods of operation are examined to verify their validity — these comprise some of the basic elements of good public relations. The library that views itself as a "cultural citadel," as one library director stated publicly, is likely to be in for a nasty shock. The community won't storm the citadel; they will simply vote down the budget (as they did in that case).

Many libraries have been carried along for years by the initial pride and enthusiasm of the community for this visible symbol of cultural maturity. Real estate brokers who haven't read a book in twenty years point proudly to the public library as a community asset. Young people are advised to drop in at the public library for college catalogs, career information, a "good" book. Senior citizens are told that the library will help them put meaning into their declining years. But does this parade of platitudes have any real meaning? Will the young adult remember favorably treatment he received at his public library? Or will he remember slights, snubs, and suspicion so that when he can cast his vote on a library budget or bond issue it will reflect his own negative experiences? Did the senior citizen in his *rising* years find the library a meaningful help so that as other pleasures and activities fade he knows it can provide a source of creative enjoyment for him? Why hasn't the real estate broker been into the library in all those years?

Unaware of the subtle changes occurring daily in the communities they would serve — or unwilling to face the fact that such changes are occurring — libraries express tremendous surprise when they encounter defeat at the hands of the public. Then, in haste and hurt, they attempt to remedy a disorder that has been building up for many years.

Alexis de Tocqueville, in his book *Democracy in America*, explains very cogently the progress by which love grows cold and loyalties erode:

> Time, events, or the unaided individual action of the mind will sometimes undermine or destroy an opinion, without any outward sign of the change. It has not been openly assailed, no conspiracy has been formed to make war on it, but its followers one by one noiselessly secede; day by day a few of them abandon it, until at

last it is only professed by a minority. In this
state it will still continue to prevail. As its enemies remain mute or only interchange their
thoughts by stealth, they are themselves unaware for a long period that a great revolution
has actually been effected; and in this state of
uncertainty they take no steps; they observe
one another and are silent. The majority have
ceased to believe what they believed before,
but they still affect to believe, and this empty
phantom of public opinion is strong enough to
chill innovators and to keep them silent and at a
respectful distance.*

Innovators in the library field have been chilled, silent
and respectful in many cases until the roof fell in. Then to them
is assigned the painful task of picking up the pieces and trying
to rebuild the structure with outdated or damaged materials.
But public confidence and affection have been seriously under-
mined, and since these are fundamental to an institution dependent upon public goodwill for its existence (people can live
without a public library, much as we would like to convince our-
selves otherwise), the reconstruction becomes an arduous and
prolonged undertaking.

The mobility of today's population is a commonplace.
The rural resident of Georgia yesterday is in metropolitan Chi-
cago today. The sophisticated New York executive will be transferred tomorrow to open a new branch office in the Middle West.
In many areas, population mobility exceeds 10 percent annually.
This does not mean, of course, that in ten years there will be a
100 percent change in the population of a given area. It does,
however, mean that no public institution can feel secure that its
message has been permanently received, because each year one
person out of ten may never have heard that message at all.

Population mobility has very serious public relations
implications for public libraries. Standards of service may vary

*Democracy in America, Henry Reeve text, rev.
by Francis Bowen (New York: Vintage Books,
1954), 2:276.

widely from one area to another. The New York executive may be greatly disappointed with his midwestern library without understanding any of the problems it is facing because nobody has bothered to brief him. The Georgian, unused to nearby library service, may not even inquire where the local public library is located. The newcomer will inevitably bring with him the background of satisfactions or disappointments which characterized his previous experience. Thus, his initial affectionate regard or hostility may not be occasioned by anything the local public library has done. But if the local public library has become ingrown, callous, or indifferent to the changes occurring in its area, an aggregate of individuals with previously unsatisfactory library experiences can affect the delicate balance of community opinion so that the scales begin to dip unfavorably. Libraries everywhere have a solemn, mutual responsibility to enhance their individual images to the end that the total image conjured up by the word *library* shall be lustrous.

The arts of public relations are both preventive and curative. The best public relations consists in developing such a sensitivity to the ambience of the library that the slightest alteration in the total design, whether internally or externally caused, will produce an inquisitive alertness upon the part of the trustees and library director plus a willingness to make necessary adjustments in patterns and plans. The second best type of public relations is "heading them off at the pass" — using proven techniques to ameliorate some undesirable situation and thus forestall an open skirmish. The least desirable type of public relations is a salvage operation after the library has suffered a defeat in the arena of public opinion.

It is incumbent upon the trustees and the director to work together to decide honestly: (1) Where is the library today in terms of effective, widespread service and adequate support based on public understanding? and (2) Where should the library be ten years from now? The bridge between the analytical answer to the first question and the optimistic answer to the second is a well-conceived public relations program, conscientiously carried out.

2

EXAMINING THE IMAGE

The words "public image" tend to be distasteful to a number of people. They conjure up visions of Madison Avenue agency men running things up flagpoles to see who salutes — librarywise, that is. Nothing could be further from the truth. Referring to Webster we find that, among other definitions, an *image* is "a mental representation of anything not actually present to the senses . . . an idea." Surely, no one could object to examining what kind of image or mental picture the general public has of the local library. How did the public form this picture anyway? Has it any basis in reality? Seeking answers to these questions is vital to establishing and continuing a good public relations program. Self-knowledge is the beginning of wise planning.

The methods of assessing local public opinion which are open to the library are diversified. They include community-wide mailings, random sampling, telephone interviews, man-on-the-street spot checks. No single method is infallible; some are quite costly and others misleading. Nevertheless, frank evaluation of the library's current status in the collective thinking of the community — its public image — is a *must* prior to launching a well-conceived public relations program. If this evaluation is to be sound, it cannot be confined to library patrons. It must in some fashion embrace a representation of the entire community. The nonuser, if not an actual "no" voter, can by his apathy increase the apparent strength of the negative element in the community. It is imperative to know who these nonusers are and what underlies their indifference to the library.

Before asking the public any questions, however, the trustees and library director must ask themselves some questions. First, will we believe the answers when we get them? In other words, how sizable a segment of responses will be convincing as far as the board and the administration are concerned? If fifteen hundred questionnaires are mailed out and 50 percent are returned and of those respondents 42 percent want bus service to the library, is the board of trustees going to agree that this is a reliable sampling and take action? If a series of telephone interviews indicates that Thursday night openings are desirable, how willing is the library director to try to schedule staff accordingly? The library must honestly determine ahead of time what its active response will be to each question it asks, whether the answer is pleasing or not.

Second, who is going to help frame the questions so that unbiased answers are received? Of course, there are professional opinion sampling firms, both large and small, and in some libraries employing such specialists may be the right step. Here, once again, the opinion sampler will ask what it is that the library wants to find out. A simple "I find the library service satisfactory — Yes/No" type of question is almost valueless. Degree of satisfaction and frequency of satisfaction are also exceedingly important. The same holds true of such a question as "Do you use the library frequently/infrequently?" The response "infrequently" may not indicate lack of interest in the library. It may indicate lack of access to public transportation.

A nearby university may be willing to assign graduate students through its sociology or social psychology department to construct a reliable questionnaire for the public library. Many schools of library science require theses for the master's degree. These schools also may be willing to assign mature students to conduct and tabulate a public opinion survey for the library. Within the community served by the library there may be individuals with expertise in opinion sampling who will volunteer their service if the need is made known. And, of course, there are books on the subject.

The manpower involved in handling an opinion sampling may deter some libraries from undertaking one. The mechanics of the survey are a legitimate project for a Friends of the Library group *if one exists*. But a Friends group should not be organized for the sole purpose of conducting an opinion poll. (Standing armies have a way of becoming an embarrassment. Friends of the Library only remain friendly when they have continuing constructive responsibilities.) Instead, a citizens' task force, with specific assignments in connection with the survey, should be organized, its services accepted, and its members discharged when the project is completed. Often prominent, busy people will cooperate on such an opinion survey if they know exactly what is expected of them and how much time they are expected to give.

Another alternative is to ask concerned local groups such as the American Association of University Women, the League of Women Voters, the Federation of Women's Clubs to assist the library. Because of its nature, the library can frequently call upon nonpartisan community groups for help whereas other more narrowly specialized institutions could not. Psychiatry has conditioned many of us to think of self-examination as a desirable thing. The library should not hesitate to ask for assistance in its efforts at self-evaluation vis-à-vis the public. Most individuals will view this as a highly commendable activity.

In opinion sampling the ultimate goal of the questioners is not to determine whether or not people like the library, but whether they understand its goals and are in sympathy with them. Many women like mink coats, but they find the price tag high. So it may be with the local public library. A favorable response in terms of thinking the library is a great place does not necessarily carry the correlative that the taxpayer is willing to foot the bill for more of the same.

In fact, opinion samplers should be wary of the "acceptable" answer in contrast to the "honest" answer. Lack of money has long been a convenient excuse for libraries which have not faced up squarely to their problems and to their deteriorating relationships with their patrons. When budget after budget is defeated or bond issues do not pass, the easy answer is "lack of money." The author has found in the majority of situations where she has been called in as a consultant that money is not the *real* answer. It is the "acceptable" answer.

If the public library is ill supported, this is a symptom, *not* a cause. One of the uses of opinion sampling is to uncover some honest answers relative to public reluctance to pay for adequate library service.

The author is acquainted with a library which has had a five-year struggle to get its budget passed. In New York State, if the library budget fails, the library may operate on the previous year's budget since it is presumed by law to be the level at which the taxpayers wish to support the library. Thus, the community cannot put its library out of business by refusing to increase the budget, but a library can certainly be killed by attrition. In the face of steadily rising costs for books, supplies, and personnel, a budget that has been static for five years can be the death knell for a library. Now, I am convinced that this library's problems lie not in the inability of the community to pay, but in the unwillingness of the community to pay for the *kind* of service it is receiving.

For example, I talked with the director at one point and asked him if he had much trouble with turnover in personnel since people like to see familiar faces when they enter the library. He assured me he holds his personnel very well because he schedules the professionals from 9 to 5 five days a week. Of course, the library doesn't open until 10 o'clock in the morning, and this is a commuter town where the only time a businessman could use his library would be after about 7:30 in the evening or on Saturday. What kind of library service is the businessman — who is also a budget voter — receiving?

A professional reference librarian is on duty in the evenings. I chatted with him and he reluctantly admitted that there are times when *ten* people are standing in line waiting for his help. Frankly, if I were number ten, I would turn on my heel and leave the library.

This library has not proved responsive to the use patterns of the community and the community is retaliating in the only way it knows how — by defeating the budget. Individual citizens, or even a group of citizens, would find it hard to give the library a bill of particulars about their dissatisfactions. Thus, it is easier for them and the library director and the board of trustees to say, "This community can't afford good library service." The basic question is: When did they last get good library service?

In addition to sampling the opinion of the community at large with the recognized instruments of polls, questionnaires, and interviews, the library trustees and the director need to ascertain who are the opinion makers in the community. It takes a discerning eye to perceive the prime movers in the power structure. Never fool yourself that the front man is the real man who is influential in his church, his lodge, his community. Librarians cannot afford to dissociate themselves from the areas where they work. They must recognize the fact that subconsciously to many people the library may represent everything they are not. It may stand for the *establishment* (whatever that term means to them) and as such be suspect. The trustees presumably represent the community on a direct basis. But when one encounters self-perpetuating boards of trustees composed of some individuals who have served for between twenty and thirty years, one wonders how in touch they are with the current scene and whether or not the answers their friends give them about the library are honest or "acceptable." Both the director and the trustees have an inescapable commitment to move out into the community, to feel its pulse, and to become familiar with the body politic.

Intimate knowledge of a community, its power structure, and its opinion makers will enable the library to estimate
in advance possible behind-the-scenes resistance to bond and
budget issues and not to blunder blindly ahead.

A specific case illustrates the point. In a wealthy and
well-established community, a conscientious board of library
trustees decided to place before the taxpayers a proposition to
erect a new building on library-owned land across the street from
the old building and to dismantle the existing dilapidated structure to provide an urgently needed parking field. It was an
intelligent, well-conceived plan and it met with the most unre-
mitting opposition from the community and finally an ignomini-
ous defeat. These are the facts, completely devoid of their
emotional content. Now for the real story.

The old library building was a memorial erected after
World War I as a community meetinghouse. Although completely
unsuited to its present tenants, the building is regarded af-
fectionately by local residents who admire its quaint exterior.
The library is situated near a complex of the Town Hall and a
Victorian-style church, bordering on a picturesque park complete
with a lake and swans. The community, resisting the inroads of
developers, has taken great pride in its few remaining historic
buildings. A society exists for their preservation. No matter how
advantageous it would have been to erect a new library and have
safe and adequate parking facilities (the existing ones are limited
and hazardous), the local residents did not feel that the prof-
fered solution was the right one for their town. At no time was
it suggested that the community did not need a new modern
library or that the proposed cost was too high. Money was not
the reason. Sentiment, emotional attachment, pride of place —
these were the heavyweights in the scale.

It took the board of trustees and the director eighteen
months to work out an alternative, but they found a solution
that won by the largest number of votes ever cast for any proposition in that community. To an outsider it sounds like something from *Alice in Wonderland*. The trustees arranged to have
the village hall moved from behind the old library building to
the vacant land across the street. They then had an architect

and engineers determine how to preserve the facade of the old building while adding eleven thousand square feet in the rear where the village hall had been. This was what the community wanted and they cheerfully voted a bond issue which was only five thousand dollars less than the original proposition to erect a completely new structure.

What is the moral of this anecdote? If the trustees of that library had been more aware of the temper of their community, of its attachment, however unreasonable, to the existing structure, they would from the beginning have proposed the type of library building local residents wanted and were willing to pay for. It needs to be stressed once again that from the beginning, money was never the problem. How the money was to be spent was the real problem and when this was properly dealt with, success was assured.

Fortified with accurate statistics about the kind of community the library serves — its size; level of education; ethnic, racial, and religious composition; the age of its residents; number of one-family and multiple dwellings and similar data — plus an honest assessment of the library's public image — the trustees and the director can proceed to formulate a public relations program of sensible scope and realistic goals.

3

RETAIN, RECRUIT, REGAIN

The very name "Public Library" sometimes lulls us into a false estimate of our status in the community and of the drawing power we assume libraries exert. No library has a single public — a large, undifferentiated group of patrons. Each library has many "publics" which it is serving with a greater or lesser degree of success. After assessing the general community attitude toward the library, the trustees, the director and the staff need to examine very closely three large patron categories — the people they are currently serving, those whom they used to serve, and those whom they have never reached. The 3 Rs of their efforts should be to retain the patrons they have, recruit new patrons, and regain lost patrons.

Naturally, the group most easily identified are those people making use of the library at the present time. Why bother to analyze them? They are already borrowers and friends. But are they? Current patrons may be divided very roughly into two groups — "captive users" and "self-propelled users."

Bulking large among captive users are students. Material for required reading assignments, answers to simple reference questions, magazines in periodical files, assistance with in-depth research work — all of these library resources and services are heavily used by students from about the fourth grade through graduate school. The school library tends to be limited in scope and heavily curriculum-oriented. It also usually closes at the end of the school day. While college and university libraries frequently possess magnificent collections, many institutions in metropolitan areas have large commuting student populations whose lives are centered off-campus. Such students, often with part-time jobs or full-time families, turn to off-campus sources for the materials they need for assignments.

A new type of college-level student, moreover, may soon be appearing at public libraries in increasing numbers — those who are enrolled in open-university programs with no attendance requirements for full college-level credit. In New York State, for example, it is expected that by 1973 regional learning centers will be located within reasonable traveling distance for any adult wishing to take up to fifteen credits toward an associate's degree or thirty credits toward a bachelor's degree. These students, wholly off-campus, may enroll at any time during the year and proceed at their own pace. Supposedly they will be provided with the A/V aids, taped lectures, films, and other media pertinent to their courses. Noncirculating books are to be available at the campus of the State University of New York with which the regional center is affiliated. Fine! if it works. But many adult students might prefer to turn to a public library which is only five blocks from home instead of to a regional center fifty miles away for the supplementary materials they need in their studies. Individuals who have developed a taste for learning late in life or whose opportunities for educational ad-

College students may find multiple uses for a public library.

vancement have been limited by external pressures can become loyal library patrons. The public libraries, however, will have to purchase promptly the materials these students will need and to publicize the fact that a nearby library is ready to support independent study programs with supplementary materials.

Of course, the privately supported university is suffering financial woes along with other institutions and in some instances can no longer supply the quantity (or breadth) of material required by its students. In the richest county in New York State (and probably one of the richest in the entire nation), the private universities are already discussing pooling their library resources and offering free access to their collections to all students irrespective of where they are enrolled. The same universities are also urging upon the county the funding and construction of a central reference library to acquire and house the more esoteric types of materials which they feel they can no longer afford to purchase or to accommodate.

Thus, a library which finds upon an honest evaluation that a sizable proportion of its existing patrons are students has no reason for self-congratulation. This is not to imply that such a group does not require intelligent assistance, a well-chosen collection, and adequate facilities for library usage. It does imply that the teenager, indifferently pursuing a school assignment, needs to be turned into a lifelong library user while we can still get our hands on him. And this is where libraries fail. Librarians often are resentful of the student user with his insistent and ill-articulated demands. The library staff, failing totally to view these young people as tomorrow's adults who can support the library or doom it, offers grudging service and impatient answers. The author has actually overheard a high-school-age patron say, "Oh, I'll wait till the nice lady is at the desk before I ask for help." The "nice lady" turns out to be a librarian who is simply according the youthful user the same degree of courtesy and polite patience she would extend to his father and mother.

Who can change staff attitudes towards students or at least modify them? This job rests squarely with the director and he is shirking his duty if he is not doing it. Directors cannot concern themselves only with book selection or attending local service club luncheons. They should be out on the floor at least a portion of each day getting the "feel" of how things are going. The best public libraries in terms of tone and staff attitude are those in which patrons *know who the director is.* Unless the director of any but the largest of city libraries can say that a regular patron in his library would recognize him, something is radically wrong. The plea of "administrative detail" is once again the acceptable rather than the honest answer, in many cases. Having achieved a directorship, how many individuals feel that they have been excused from further on-the-floor responsibilities and act accordingly?

This is not to suggest that a director is a super-sleuth, silently checking up on his staff. He is there to reinforce their efforts, to take on the difficult patron, to protect the staff from the afternoon onslaught of forty students arriving all at once on

Wherever reading interest develops, libraries should capitalize on it.

the library bus. When a disgruntled patron demands to see the director because he has had to wait too long for a reserve book, resents the amount of his fine, or objects to "that" book being in the library at all, staff members need to know that the director is ready to back them up and to relieve the pressure on them — certainly to remove the problem from the public arena of the circulation desk. A procedure should be established for the handling of complaints and every staff member should be well informed as to what that procedure is. (ALA has published a helpful leaflet entitled "Count on Complaints" which deals succinctly with this subject.)

Staff members who are convinced that their superior knows the problems they face in dealing with student patrons will usually be far more sympathetic toward this captive group than those who feel that "he" is never around when "they" are making use of the library.

Why all this emphasis on the student patron? Because, like the adult who must deal with public utilities, the student has no choice but to use the public library. Whatever our individual level of frustration with the telephone company, our recourse is limited. In much the same way, whatever treatment the student is receiving in his public library, there isn't too much he can do about it — except to remember. At another time, in another place, his recollection of unhappy library experiences in the past may provide the unconscious motivation for his negative vote on a library referendum. With the increasing mobility of population mentioned in chapter 1, no public library can afford to treat its student population with indifference or lack of concern. The attitude displayed is like a stone dropped in the water; the librarian cannot know what distant shore the ripple will reach.

Of course, a sizable number of library patrons come in because they have personal reasons for using what the library has to offer. The businessman wants to consult a specialized directory. The homemaker has decided to reupholster a chair. The minister wants to do some research on flowers mentioned in the Bible. These are the "self-propelled" users and they should form the backbone of library support — its mainstay whatever the financial and political climate. How is this segment of the library's public welcomed and served?

When was the last time the director and the trustees looked at their library through the eyes of a patron? The author recalls entering one building where it seemed to her that the chairs and tables were arranged very peculiarly so that they were not directly below the overhead source of light. She asked the reason for this and the director replied, "It gives us better surveillance." Persistent inquiries revealed that the director estimated that one patron out of a thousand was mutilating or stealing books. Thus, nine hundred and ninety-nine desirable patrons were daily inconvenienced by poor physical arrangements and bad lighting to circumvent one undesirable patron with larcenous tendencies. This is a bad ratio and the director admitted it.

The conversation and the director's subsequent rethinking of the problem resulted in the redesign of the entire

main floor of the building to provide both patron comfort and adequate surveillance.

The self-propelled patron should never be taken for granted. He has his limits of tolerance for a shabby setting, lack of amicability on the part of the staff, too little breadth and depth in the book collection. It will be disastrous for this library when such once-loyal patrons begin to "noiselessly secede."

Look at the bulletin boards, the display cases, the lounge areas. How would they strike you if you had never visited your library before? Do they convey a sense of lively activity, pleasant welcome, a "with it" aura, or do they perpetuate the stereotype of the library as a dingy place populated by individuals more interested in preserving the books than in serving the patrons? If you can't manage to have a good-looking community bulletin board, don't have one. A tacky collection of outdated announcements is no recommendation for the library. If you cannot assign personnel to change the display cases on a regular basis, seriously consider soliciting outside professional help. One library has a collection of carved birds which had been in the display case so long that a matte knife was required to loosen their feet from the shelf. This library also owns antique dolls, original artwork from children's classics, irresistible old-fashioned valentines, and many more treasures — none of which were displayed because the birds were so valuable that no one wanted to touch them. This is not the function of library display cases. A library is not a museum and should not accept gifts of such value and rarity that the staff is afraid of them. The genuine purpose of displays and exhibits will be discussed in a subsequent chapter.

How about lounge facilities? Can a patron in your library sit down and browse through a book or magazine before he checks it out? Many libraries feel they are too small or too overcrowded to provide this amenity. If that is true, perhaps the time for expansion has come. If it is not true, look around your plant with a critical eye. Decide whether furniture, shelves, book trucks, and other impedimenta are in their present locations because a quarter of a century ago the architect planned it that way or because these locations and arrangements really meet patrons' needs today. Even such a seemingly drastic step as cutting a door through a wall may be indicated to improve the traffic flow for library use as it has emerged.

Many libraries were built before microfilm reader-printers became the commonplace they are today. Other reference facilities may have diminished in importance over the years with the increased popularity of microfilm. Is your library arranged so that patrons can comfortably use this new and vital adjunct or has the microfilm section merely been jammed in with little regard for its growing importance to patrons? Human nature resists change and librarians are no different from other human beings. But if they want to hold onto the patrons they already have, they are going to have to revamp their ways of doing business at the library to accommodate these VIPs better than ever before.

How does a would-be patron find your library? Are there clear directional signs on the main access streets? Is the building itself labeled "library"? This may sound like a foolish question, but older libraries, those in smaller communities, and those just getting started are sometimes located in former homes, office buildings, and even stores, so that the casual passerby or the determined seeker may not at once recognize the building for what it is. Is the library adequately illuminated at night, including the parking area? Are the hours posted in some conspicuous place, visible from the outside of the building, so that if a potential patron arrives when the library is closed, he can easily find out when to return? On a rainy day what do you want a borrower to do with his dripping umbrella? Do you provide shopping bags (plainly identified as being supplied by the library) in which he can place his books, magazines, and records to protect them from ruin in the rain? If one library cannot afford such bags or cannot use the minimum quantity the fabricator insists upon, usually a few telephone calls to neighboring libraries will generate sufficient interest to make the purchase feasible for everyone.

How about the handicapped person who may want to use your library? Is there any door wide enough to admit a wheelchair? If your library has forbidding front steps, could a ramp be constructed leading to a side door not generally used by the public? One library deliberating how to locate such a ramp for maximum convenience, very nearly found itself the recipient of some very bad publicity when the local newspaper editor, stirred up by a single family with a handicapped child, began to question why in an annual operating budget of over $500,000 the Board of Trustees could not locate $1,000 to pay for such a ramp. Fortunately, many years of carefully cultivated good relations with the editor stood the library in good stead. When it was explained to him that the Board was working on the problem, he gave them full credit in his news columns. He also kept a sharp eye on that library to be sure that the ramp was actually built. Naturally, the first people invited to use the ramp were the parents of the handicapped child. A near crisis was turned into the best kind of public relations.

If a newcomer does manage to locate the library and arrives when it is open, what kind of welcome does he receive? Every library should have a simple, good-looking informational

folder for new patrons. This folder should be friendly in tone. (One library was finally persuaded to discard its "welcoming" leaflet which quoted verbatim the sections of municipal law having to do with stealing books and damaging library property.) The folder should contain information about borrowing privileges (how many books, magazines, records); fines and fees; special collections (large-print books, talking books, microfilm); unusual regulations (magazines do not circulate until four weeks after the date of issue); special events (story hours, adult programs, motion pictures); individualized services (telephone reference, telephone renewals, assistance with bibliographies, interlibrary loan, reserves), and an indication that the library is one of the few places in the community geared to serve all ages and all levels of interest. If the library is a multilevel one or has a complex building, floor plans should be included. Such a folder should be made available to the Welcome Wagon in the community. It could be placed in the offices of real estate brokers, pediatricians, and insurance agents and on the counters of banks and utility companies. In other words, information about the library should be available in places newcomers will be most likely to visit when they first move into the area. If someone arrives in your area with a mental block about libraries, such a folder will be a good first step toward improving his attitude.

Of course, no library can rely on passersby walking in off the street as its only method of recruiting new library patrons. No merchant expects to stay in business solely through the customers he can attract by his window displays. Techniques of bringing people into the library are discussed in chapters 5-8. Suffice it to say that when someone finally does take the big step through the front door (and for many people it is a big step because the library is a symbol of a society in which they have not always felt welcome), everyone on the staff should be well prepared to receive him.

In addition to the informational leaflet, some libraries provide the new registrant with a kit of helpful materials. These can include the most recent reading lists and bookmarks issued by the library, an invitation to join the Friends of the Library if such a group exists, specific dates and hours of programs currently presented at the library, a short history of the library, facts about the library building if it is unique in some way, a leaflet on how to use the card catalog, a simplified version of the Dewey Decimal System. The new recruit to the ranks of library users leaves the library feeling as if he has done something quite special by taking out a library card. In point of fact, he has.

The saddest and most difficult public to reach is comprised of former patrons who no longer use the library. What alienated them? In some ways, a library director should be grateful to the patron who loudly lodges a complaint. At least in this case, he knows what has gone wrong and can make conciliatory motions. The patron who expresses his dissatisfaction first by staying away and then by voting No on bond and budget issues is a far more dangerous and difficult foe. He no longer believes in what he once supported and the library does not know what made him change his mind.

Rekindling interest in the library on the part of former patrons is a very slow process. It will never be possible to win everyone back because some individuals like to nurse their grievances and they are happy to hate you (the establishment). In certain cases, the library director and his staff can make some shrewd educated guesses at the cause of an alienation of affection. Sometimes "bigness" is in itself a problem. The patron who enjoyed the library when it was located in a corner store may not feel nearly so much at home in the handsome new building of which everyone is so proud. Librarians need to be alert to keep their services as individualized as possible after a move to larger quarters. The shy as well as the self-important patron may feel put off by the new larger surroundings and gradually drift away.

Conversely, "smallness" may have been the library's problem when it was in its formative years with a limited collection and inadequate physical facilities. Patrons may have drifted away from the library because "they never have what I want" or because the noise level and crowded conditions were distasteful to them. Once the library is located in larger quarters, every effort must be made to inform the entire community of what awaits the borrower in the new building (space, light, silence, improved collections, a browsing area) and in this way win back lost patrons.

Another cause of disaffection may be a change in hours of service inadequately explained to the patron who suddenly finds himself inconvenienced or disrupted from his habitual pattern of library use. Changes such as this should have widespread advance publicity and be adequately explained in order to achieve as much patron acceptance *before the fact* as possible.

Less easy to reach or mollify is the patron who feels he has been the victim of an injustice due to the library's overzealous interpretation of some regulation. Many patrons erroneously believe that they are entitled to overdue notices. Actually, it is their moral and legal responsibility to return the books they have borrowed and the overdue notice is merely a customary courtesy on the part of the library. When such a notice fails to go out through some mischance and a patron discovers a book behind the couch which is six months overdue, he is furious at the library for not reminding him to bring it back. Although such an occurrence cannot be circumvented entirely, it might help if it were plainly indicated on overdue notices that this is a courtesy of the library and not a patron's right. At least, this would give the director some leverage when an angry patron confronts him and refuses to pay the fine.

The same type of public relations problem arises when a patron claims he has returned a book which the library cannot locate. Humility on the library's part will do a lot toward helping the situation. Books are misshelved and library employees do forget. Some procedure which permits a reasonable amount of time to elapse (three months, perhaps) in which one party or the other may find the book is good public relations. Afterwards, many libraries are willing to "split the difference" and pay half of the cost of the book since to be righteously right and lose a patron is a Pyrrhic victory.

Library regulations often seem senseless to patrons, and if the rules are too rigorously enforced with only grudging explanations given, there is bound to be resentment, as the following incident shows. Attempting to get a book on horsemanship for one of her children, a library patron was informed by the clerk at the circulation desk, "We don't take reserves on children's books." Asked why not, the clerk said, "It's our policy." In this case the patron went to the director to ask for an explanation. What he told her made good sense and was eminently satisfactory: reserves on children's books don't pay off. Either the child ignores the notice when it arrives or he lacks transportation to the library to pick up the book before the reserve has expired, and he is exceedingly disappointed if the book is not waiting for him when he finally appears. In other words, reserves on children's books cause more headaches than they cure. How simple for the clerk to have offered this explanation — *if she knew it*. And this is the sticking point. Library personnel come and go and it is incumbent upon the director or the personnel officer to be sure that a parrot-like recitation of the regulations is not the extent of the new employee's in-service training. If there isn't a sensible reason for a policy or if the policy has not been reexamined for a very long time, the director and the administrative staff are in for some very serious public relations problems.

Some libraries, of course, have difficult people on the staff who are ill suited to deal with the public. The present director may have inherited them or he may have made a mistake in his selection of personnel. Illness, family problems, a longing for "the good old days" — many things may be contributing to the individual's soured outlook on life. But, if at all possible, he must not be permitted to inflict his dissatisfaction with society on library patrons. In a sense, patrons are defenseless. They can shout back, but this won't help them get the material they need. A short-tempered clerk, an indifferent reference librarian, a children's librarian who doesn't much care for children any more — such individuals erode the library's image and present major public relations problems.

There is no pat solution for such problems. Tactful counseling, a leave of absence, compassionate sick leave, or just a plain old-fashioned scolding may sometimes help. Or the director may have to reshuffle his staff so that the ill-natured person is in contact with the public as little as possible. In extreme cases it may be necessary for the Board of Trustees to intervene and place the individual on probation. None of this is pleasant, but affronts to patrons aren't pleasant either and they will retaliate in the only way they know how — by staying away and by voting No if they have the opportunity.

The leverage for good or ill which a single patron can exercise is demonstrated by the following hypothetical but perfectly plausible anecdote. A blue-collar worker, diffident, uncertain, a trifle embarrassed, stops in at his public library to get a book on automobile repair. Staring indifferently at him, the clerk at the desk says, in response to his question about where such books are located, "Look it up in the card catalog." Unwilling to say that he doesn't know how to use the card catalog, the would-be patron shuffles around in the aisles for a while and returns home empty-handed. His wife asks him, "Where is the book on car repair?" Unwilling to admit that he couldn't find the book because of his lack of expertise in using the library, the man says, "What a rotten library! They don't have any books at all on car repair."

The next day the wife's sister stops by and says, "When is Jack going to repair that car of yours? I thought he was going to get a book about it at the public library." To which, of course, the wife replies that the library doesn't have any books on the subject. That night at dinner the sister tells the story to her husband, a taxi driver. The following day, the taxi driver turns to his passenger as they are passing the public library and says, "What a rotten library! My brother-in-law couldn't even get a book on how to repair his car." The passenger happens to be a member of the Board of Aldermen and the next time the library budget is discussed, he denounces the miserably equipped public library that buys dirty books and a lot of highbrow trash and neglects the solid citizens of the community. And the library director is completely mystified about the genesis of this seemingly unprovoked attack. Thus do very small Davids bring very large Goliaths to their knees.

4

MEETING PATRONS' NEEDS

A library is basically in the book business. All of the other adjuncts to library service which make a library the multimedia communications center so readily praised by library personnel and so little understood by patrons are subordinate to the book collection. It makes no difference whether the books are in hard cover or paperback, on microfilm, microfiche, or microdot — the fact remains that the average library user thinks of his library card primarily as entitling him to read and borrow books. He may be delighted to find that his library has a good record collection, can obtain films for his use, will lend him a fine art reproduction for his home, and can provide tapes with cassettes to play them on. But none of these supplementary features will seem important (or even worth-while) to him if he can't find the book he wants. Ingrained in the public consciousness is the idea that the core, the heart, the very essence of a library is *books*. Over many generations the library profession may be able to modify and broaden this concept, and certainly some progress has been made in this direction with the general acceptance of records and films as having a rightful place in the library. However, as recently as 1969 the weekly newspaper in a wealthy suburb of New York City bitterly criticized the local public library for expanding its record collection because "everybody in this community owns a fine record collection." The educational job of interpreting the multimedia library is obviously far from complete.

If the average patron is looking (or thinks he is looking) for a book, what are the public relations implications of this mental set? First, the library director and his trustees must refer to the analysis of their community which was recommended in chapter 2. Has there been a major shift in population? Older? Younger? Of different racial or ethnic composition? Is the economic level of the area served by the library on an upward or downward spiral? Are patterns of employment changing? Are young executives moving in or moving out? What percentage of high school graduates are college-bound? What happens to the non-college-bound graduate? If the library is to augment its book collection on the basis of the publics which it hopes to serve, questions such as these, and many more, equally penetrating, must be asked and answered.

One of the most prestigious metropolitan libraries in the nation is currently undergoing a searching evaluation of its entire policy structure because within a decade over half of those whom it will serve will be black. In this inner-city library, whose former patrons now live in the outer-ring suburbs, the library director and his staff know that a business-as-usual philosophy will eventually put them out of business for lack of patrons and, by extension, for lack of public support through the city council. How to revamp their personnel policies, their book purchases, the hours of service, the location of branches, the image of that great and powerful library in the eyes of the people who will ultimately constitute over 50 percent of its potential patrons — these questions are currently being studied by the library administration. They are charting a ten-year course of action before the fact, not waiting until the debacle and then trying to piece together some viable library service.

Unfortunately, most libraries, whether large or small, are unwilling to look ahead and plan accordingly. Dropping circulation figures are a common complaint on the library scene. Actually, they have never been the reliable yardstick of use which everyone liked to believe. A book taken out by one member of a family may be read by three other people before it is returned, and still only one circulation is recorded. The patron who wants to identify a line from an old poem which keeps running through her head is just as pleased if the library can locate the quotation for her as the borrower of a best seller. Who can say which individual experienced the highest level of patron satisfaction and has become the more enthusiastic supporter of the library? Nevertheless, when it is evident that a serious drop in circulation is continuing, certainly the director, his staff, and the board of trustees ought to feel that something is wrong. A warning bell is ringing.

A library serving a new housing development may need to stock far more "how to" books on patio construction and gardening than a library in a more established suburb. Certainly, the urban dweller will have comparatively little use for such books (although he might like to know how to make a dish garden or how to repair a leaking faucet that the landlord ignores). Too often in the name of having a well-rounded collection, books with little relevance to the library service area *as it has evolved* are purchased or remain on the shelves, crowding out the more meaningful titles for which the patron is looking.

The author is convinced that basic to the severe troubles (almost persecution) experienced by one director in a widely publicized situation was the fact that the Board of Trustees contained no representation of the newer elements in the community which had changed markedly in character over a twenty-year period. From a semirural setting of older homes populated by families who knew each other from "way back when," the community has become urbanized, with small factory

Storefront libraries in Washington, D.C., put the library where the action is. Mayor Walter E. Washington accepted an honorary card.

enclaves, with blue-collar workers, semi-skilled professionals and disadvantaged people, both black and white, occupying small development-style houses. Little effort was made to change the library's pattern of operation during the years when it was plain to see that the community itself was changing. Board members were reelected term after term without opposition. On the surface, there were no ripples. But underneath, the gap between the library and the community was widening. The situation needed only a catalyst in the form of a demagogue who could accuse the library of wasting taxpayers' money on "filth" to blow off the lid.

A fundamental question has remained unanswered as far as the author is concerned: In a community hard pressed to pay its taxes, how justified was the library director in purchasing an esoteric magazine of interest to a handful of people? Didn't this library set the stage for its own crisis? Wouldn't it have been better to tell the few people who wanted this highly specialized magazine that the library couldn't afford it and to purchase an additional subscription to some magazine in demand in the community? In the furor over intellectual freedom which has surrounded the case, the right of a community to question how its tax dollars are being spent has been almost entirely overlooked. While libraries cannot be run like old-fashioned town meetings, with everyone having his say, trustees sensitive to the changing structure of a community should reflect concern for how well the library is meeting emerging patterns of patron use.

The book-collection issue does not have to be as inflammatory as censorship; it can be one of common sense and even of the director having a personal preference for certain subject matter. One library in a community which is populated largely by retirees in the winter and by beach-house homeowners in the summer, has a superb collection of law books because the erstwhile director found them interesting. The new director, by outfitting a rolling cart with an umbrella and tape-recorded music, has taken the library out onto the boardwalk for the benefit of the bathers and the older people sitting in the sunshine. By rearranging the library, enlarging the paperback collection, introducing books in languages other than English, and responding generally to the community as it *now* exists, not as it once was — a fashionable exclusive summer resort — the director has also increased the circulation and succeeded in upping the budget which had remained static for several years. Once again, money was not the basic question. How the money was being spent was assuredly the point at issue.

Willingness to change and to experiment do not seem to have characterized the library profession. Perhaps this is because libraries were once sacrosanct and, like the flag and motherhood, no one would dare to challenge their right to exist and to continue just as they always had. In the shifting social scene this immunity to challenge is gone. Individuals (not all philistines, either) are willing to stand up in public and inveigh against library taxes. They write letters to the editor about poor service, inadequate collections, and overelaborate building plans. In one community a group organized itself and had a letterhead printed reading "Enemies of the Friends of the Library."

It is a truism that most people do not like what is good for them. Are we continuing in the library business to give patrons what we consider is good for them or are we watching out for signs of disenchantment? Patrons do not buy library service in the ordinary sense that they can freely choose to make the purchase or not. If the library is a tax-supported institution, and this is certainly the case with almost all public libraries, some portion of the individual's taxes is being used for library purposes. If he is not a taxpayer he may feel that other municipal services could be better financed if so much money were not allocated to the library.

A deteriorating library in one very wealthy community had to wait in line nearly four years while the taxpayers were asked to approve a new garage for the snowplows, an ice-skating rink, new street lighting, and better uniforms for the police force. Very few people questioned the order of priorities assigned by the village board. It was only when overcrowded conditions reached the point that book purchases had to be curtailed for lack of space that local residents began to question whether or not a new library was needed.

Library patrons do not have an overall view of the community. They know if their neighborhood is changing. They know if their husbands have had to change jobs. They know if their children use the library for school assignments. They do not necessarily know whether a wholly new pattern is emerging for the community in which they live. It is the duty of the trustees and the library director to discern and prepare for such changes.

In the Cumberland Valley — to cite a specific instance — light industry has brought professional and semiskilled workers into a formerly rural area. These newcomers live in housing developments and garden-style apartments. The library serving this area is in serious financial trouble, barely able to raise the funds required for matching state aid. An examination of the pattern of operation clearly shows that the library has continued to function exactly as if a whole segment of new people did not

Readying the bookmobile for a busy day in the suburbs.

exist. The bookmobile still runs exclusively to farming settlements; the evening hours at the library (when after-work family patronage might be expected) have not been increased; no overt effort has been made to encourage these families to become library patrons. To expect that any of them will raise a finger to help the library in its financial crisis is very optimistic indeed. And yet, the library trustees must have known for four or five years that the industrial buildings were going up, the development housing and apartments were under construction. Apparently no long-term planning was done to embrace this new and different public in the operational scheme of the library.

Library patrons are denied another privilege accorded to the individual shopping for an ordinary service or commodity. There isn't anyplace else to go. Failing to find an electric can opener to his liking in one discount store, the would-be purchaser can go to another store for what he wants. The library patron who consistently cannot find what he wants in his library has no recourse except to complain. Sometimes, through direct access, he can use a library in a neighboring community, or his home library will offer to obtain the desired material on interlibrary loan. This is a temporary solution to meet an emergency situation. But if month after month the library is turning patrons to other sources to meet their needs, something is seriously wrong.

A tiny, overburdened library feels it has a good excuse — lack of shelf space and a limited budget. A big barnlike library feels it has a good excuse — insufficient staff to help the patrons and a limited budget. In both cases, the library is attributing its difficulties to external causes. Actually the solution is within the library's own public relations activities. If the small library has truly outgrown its setting, what are the trustees and the director doing about plans for expansion? What better opportunity to talk up a new building program than when a patron complains about a book he can't find? This is a great opening for the librarian to say, "If we had a new building, we could accommodate thousands of additional books in our collection." The large metropolitan library, complaining about the lack of city funds to properly staff its branches, may have become so deeply imbedded in its rigid book acquisition setup that there is no flexibility in what the individual librarian on the local scene can select for "his people." No matter how plentiful the personnel, if the books aren't well chosen, the patron cannot be helped.

Every librarian knows that there are seasonal demands for books — gardening in the springtime, skiing in the wintertime. Gathering books on a current topic together in a conspicuous place near the circulation desk so that individuals who are interested in them can spot them immediately is a valid way of creating patron goodwill and improving circulation. Holidays, the birthdays of national heroes, local special events, and similar occasions can be observed by grouping parts of the library's collection together to make them easily accessible. Instant service is the result. A Polish-American, for example, will certainly be pleased to come into the library and find that books on Polish history, art, customs, literature, and music are being featured in honor of Kosciusko's birthday. Similarly, the League of Women Voters might like it if during election time books on politics and the political process were plainly displayed. The immediate reaction of some library directors may be, "We haven't time for that sort of thing." If so, it would be wise for each director to ask himself, "What is my staff doing eight hours a day that is more important than familiarizing our patrons with fresh aspects of our collection and encouraging them to borrow a book?" A truly lively library should be constantly at work offering its wares in as many diverting and intriguing ways as possible. But it must have the right wares on hand in the first place.

5

COMMUNICATING WITH PATRONS
THROUGH MASS MEDIA

About two thirds of the people in the United States are not making use of their public libraries. While this statement can be modified by explanatory comments — "In some sections of the country, one library has to serve four thousand square miles," or "Residential neighborhoods become industrialized and there's no one left to patronize the public library" — the fact nevertheless remains that libraries on the whole have not succeeded in getting potential patrons through the front door. If libraries believe that they are entitled to adequate support from the public treasury whether by direct or indirect taxation, they have an inescapable obligation to attract as many patrons as possible to use their facilities. *Outreach* is a common word in library parlance, but its practical applications have been somewhat limited.

In determining how to attract patrons into the library, the director, his staff, and the library trustees should first assess what channels of communication are open to them. Newspapers, radio, and television are the mass media channels through which possible patrons can be reached. But no single channel will reach everyone. No single message, however widely disseminated, will do the job. Informing the public where you are, what you have, and how it will benefit the individual patron is a continuing obligation of the library if it is to grow — and, in some cases, if it is to survive.

The most obvious channel of communication is the local newspaper, both weekly and daily. While the daily paper reaches a wider number of readers, the weekly paper often has a deeper level of penetration because the news is particularized for a given community. It is incumbent upon the library director to make the initial contact with the newspaper editor. Later on, a staff member can be designated to handle the publicity aspect of the public relations program, but initially the editor, who is the chief executive in his organization, should be approached by the director, who is the chief executive of the library. This is a professional courtesy.

The mechanics of publicity (double-spaced typing, using one side of the paper, plainly indicated release date, etc.) are covered in depth in the paperback manual by Marie D. Loizeaux, *Publicity Primer*, a classic in the field. Librarians should have a well-thumbed copy on hand. This manual also discusses the various events, activities, and occasions which can be converted into good publicity for the library. Basic to an understanding of the function of good publicity is this statement by Miss Loizeaux:

> The *only* legitimate reasons for publicizing the library upon any occasion — in print or out — are to make known library resources, to furnish information, to explain or solicit patronage, or support, and to foster good will. These are pretty inclusive, but there are certain items which not only fall outside of these categories,

> but which may be definitely detrimental to one
> or more of them. The library publicity worker's
> first task is the editing — in terms of library
> policies and precepts — of the subject matter
> to be released.*

This is a succinct policy statement for the guidance of anyone who is in anguish over whether or not to release a particular piece of news. If it's not good for the library's long-term public relations efforts, it's not good. A case in point occurred many years ago when the author was the public relations director for a major Eastern graduate school. The first black student in the history of the college was elected president of the Student Council. In those days, this was *news*. In fact, another university had recently been featured on the front page of the New York *Times* with a story about the first black captain of its football team. While she was debating how to handle the story, a delegation from the Student Council came to her office to request that no story be released at all. The gist of their plea was that the individual had been elected to the presidency because of his leadership qualities and that these were not to be confused with the color of his skin. After reflecting upon the sincerity of the students, she concluded that whatever external acclaim might redound to the college's credit, such a story would harm internal relations with the student body — a far more important public than the casual newspaper reader. The story was not released.

There is always a great temptation for the publicity person to bring the library director a scrapbook full of clippings to prove how effective the program has been. This is a very fallible yardstick. Unless the publicity is advancing the cause of good library service, it is not an integral part of the public relations program. Publicity is the handmaid of public relations and should never be allowed to get the upper hand.

This is not to suggest that bad news about the library should be suppressed. Suppression would be a fatal course, sure to undermine the newspaper's opinion of the trustworthiness of

*Publicity Primer, 4th ed., 2d ptg., (New York: H. W. Wilson Company, 1967), p. 35.

the library as a source of news. Every library has unpleasant incidents — bomb scares, molestations, robberies, indecent exposures. If the police are called in and these ugly events become part of the public record, a newspaper has every right to call the library and ask for its version of what occurred. In such cases, the reporter will probably want to speak to the director, who should not go into hiding. He should give the facts of the matter as dispassionately as possible and nothing more. He should not indulge in any "off the record" remarks, which have an uncanny way of getting on the record and into print. In a crisis, other staff members should be discouraged from talking to reporters since a single channel of communication is usually sufficient to keep the facts straight; this is all that the library should attempt when it is involved in a bad situation. A tight-lipped, "no comment" attitude will not win friends among the press and will probably result in ill will toward the library.

Usually, if good relations with the press have been developed over a period of time, the newspapers will tend to play down an unpleasant event. After all, who hasn't had a bomb scare these days? It is only when it appears to the reporter that the library is trying to cover up something that his professional determination to ferret out a story comes into full play and then the library may be in for a very hard time indeed.

An episode drawn from the experience of a major university may help to illustrate the point. A student committed suicide by jumping out of a dormitory window. It was a horrible episode and one which, of course, attracted the attention of the newspapers. With the consent of the administration, the public relations officer was able to make full details of the case available to the press. The event took place when the partition of India and Pakistan was in progress. The student was a Moslem whose family was being uprooted from its home in India and relocated in Pakistan. In the upheaval, he had lost track of his relatives. He was a nervous, troubled, difficult person. His college counselor, as well as the head of the department dealing with students from other lands, had had many conferences with him in an endeavor to reassure him about the course of his life and the safety of his family. They had been in touch with the Indian and

Pakistani consulates. All of the steps that were humanly possible had been taken, to no avail. The young man, despondent and despairing, made his tragic decision. The newspapers were satisfied with this information. The tabloids did not even bother with the story and the major nationally-read newspaper ran about three inches on an inside page. If there had been the least reluctance upon the part of the university to make known the full facts in the case, a far different treatment would surely have resulted. A grace note was a letter from the Pakistani ambassador to the United States thanking the university for its sympathetic handling of the incident.

All of the foregoing observations have been based on the assumption that the library has a friendly, working relationship with the press. But how does one handle a hostile newspaper? First, by trying to uncover the roots of the hostility. These may date back to "the bad old days" of the previous director, and the editor may assume that the slings and arrows suffered at that time are still held in readiness. The new director needs to talk to the editor and set forth his own viewpoint about relations with the newspaper. Patient, pleasant persistence may win over the editor. If the newspaper continues to attack the library in its editorial columns, the director (possibly accompanied by a trustee) should make a renewed effort to ask for *news* coverage of the library on the grounds that it is a public, tax-supported institution and news of its activities is a legitimate concern of the people in the community. Unless the editor is a very strange newspaperman, he will usually respond to this approach. The library is not trying to dictate his editorial policy, it is merely asking for news coverage of the same type accorded to any other municipal body. Above all, library people should not threaten or retaliate. A *good* library can survive ill treatment by a hostile newspaper.

Some libraries have antagonized the local newspaper by confusing it with a house organ. This is particularly true in the case of a weekly paper in which the library may mistakenly feel it has a "right" to have its material printed, and exactly as submitted at that. No matter how few the pages or how dull the text, the editor of a newspaper views it as a *news*paper and he will resent the implication that any institution has a right to space on his pages. Libraries sometimes make the mistake of always sending the best photograph to the daily or of setting release dates so that a really newsworthy story appears in the daily press several days before the publication date of the weekly. Whenever possible, the weekly should be given friendly consideration in the release of news. If a special event occurs on a date which effectively prevents the weekly from giving it news coverage, another angle should be devised from which the event can be successfully covered by the weekly. The dailies do not look upon the weeklies as competitors, but the converse is certainly true.

Libraries cannot wait complacently for news to happen if they want to keep this channel of communication open so that present and potential patrons are constantly aware of their library through the public press. Groundbreakings and gifts of Gutenberg Bibles are few and far between. *Publicity Primer* covers in detail ways to capitalize on other events from the circulation of the hundred-thousandth book to the fact that fifty local residents are listed in the latest edition of *Who's Who in America*. But library staff members need to be educated to recognize what constitutes news and to bring it to the attention of the individual responsible for doing something about it. Far better to ask whether a particular happening is news than to assume it isn't and be wrong.

Naturally, this is not to suggest that a library will indulge in manufacturing news. Nothing destroys a library's reputation as a reliable source of news faster than a faked publicity picture or a story not grounded in actual fact. But — and this is a big *but* — the skillful and creative handling of a potentially newsworthy event can turn it into something the papers will be glad to print. For example, if the library has on display a collection of campaign buttons, there is nothing wrong with inviting the local state senator down to admire the display. Library personnel looking at their own display are hardly news. An elected official amused by the style of campaigning used in bygone days presents exactly the light touch which newspapers welcome. There is nothing phony about this. The display exists in the library. The senator was invited to come and look at it. He ac-

Giant-size library card dramatizes shift to automation.

cepted the invitation and a photograph was taken. It is all perfectly straightforward. The creative touch was thinking to call
the senator in the first place.

Similarly, anniversary celebrations tend to be routine
observances with very little newspaper appeal unless some creative thinking goes into the planning. A very successful example
of building a human-interest angle into the ceremonies was the
fiftieth anniversary of a college at which all of the speakers were
the successors in office to the men and women who had spoken
at the dedication exercises a half century before. The college had
in its archives photographs taken at that dedication and copies
were made available to the newspapers. The printed program was

a replica of the one used fifty years before. Photographs of old-time classrooms with Gibson-girl students were contrasted with the modern equipment and modish attire of current students. The educators and dignitaries who spoke were given the opportunity to comment on how their own institutions had grown and changed over the intervening years. The ceremonies were a marvelous combination of nostalgia (very dear to the hearts of graduates from the early days) with a progressive look toward the future. So effective was this combination that *Life* magazine devoted a four-page spread to the event.

Radio offers an excellent channel of communication in many areas and the possibilities for air time are far better than many libraries assume. After all, in order to retain its license, a station must devote a portion of its air time to public service programs. Why shouldn't some of them be library-related? The same procedure advocated for newspapers should be followed in dealing with radio stations — an initial one-to-one contact between the library director and the station manager. This can be followed up by a brass-tacks conversation between the program director and the individual designated by the library to handle publicity in general or radio in particular.

Radio programs include interviews, theatrical reviews, round-table discussions, music, news, sports, special events coverage, and announcements. The library can fit into almost any of these categories if a creative approach characterizes the thinking of the publicity specialist. The library can, for example, offer to supply "Facts about Famous Sports Personalities," to be used by the sportscaster with a suitable acknowledgment to the public library. This is an excellent way to let the sports-minded listener know that the library has some good books on his particular sphere of interest. He might even come in and look around.

A weekly five-minute book review program may appeal to the station. The book reviews can usually be taped ahead of time and should, of course, cover a wide range of reading material in the hope of luring nonpatrons into the library. If the station has a theatre critic who covers the nearby metropolitan openings or the repertory company which comes to town, the library can usually supply him with background material about earlier versions of the play, whether it was dramatized from a book, what the original critics said — many small helps to make his broadcast more entertaining. While the critic won't give the library credit every time, he will become a genuine friend, and people in the communications field are valuable friends to have.

The library can provide radio stations with names of staff members who have interesting backgrounds or unusual hobbies suitable for interview or discussion programs. One librarian the author knows is a stunt flyer — quite a change from the stereotype of the past. Libraries are often acquainted with local authors (who may have done some of their research at the library) and can suggest them as program possibilities to the radio station. A good storyteller for children is an attraction any station would welcome. It must be understood that the radio station will not be able in every case to acknowledge its debt to the library, but when a healthy working relationship has been established, the library will be in a good position to request that some announcements of its own be put on the air. Occupational information for the man thinking about a new job; high school equivalency examination information; special records for brush-up work in shorthand; books in languages other than English; large-print books for the visually handicapped — these are some of the library services which should be publicized over the radio because this medium will reach individuals who frequently are not book-oriented. It will probably come as a revelation to the high school dropout that the public library has information about how he can get a diploma with no embarrassing questions and no recriminations.

Television is the most challenging medium, much more sophisticated in its demands than radio. Few libraries can hope to produce materials of the caliber suited to television programming. There is no harm, however, in making friendly contacts with the television stations in your area. You can offer to assist them in think-type programs which require literate people. Such an offer may be productive of worthwhile openings for library personnel or for interesting individuals whom you can suggest to the station because they are regular library patrons. If the station reserves a certain amount of time for programs which are purely local in origin, the library might present a weekly picture-book story hour. Since most libraries have an overflow of small children as patrons, this will probably not be beneficial from the point of view of attracting new borrowers, but such a program can enhance the image of the library as a friendly community institution in the minds of parents.

Television spots, of course, are visuals which cannot be prepared by the cut-and-paste technique. With rare good fortune you may find a professional in your area who will donate his photographic talents or his artistic or cartooning abilities to the production of a television spot for the library. A very big library with ample funds may have either a competent staff artist or the wherewithal to employ outside specialists. Most libraries will have to content themselves with *participation* in television programs where it is feasible. Public-service announcements for television are likely to be beyond the talent and budget resources of the average library.

An example of a more coordinated effort illustrates the effectiveness of mass media communication with patrons. In New York State in the late 1960's five neighboring public library systems cooperated in a four-year project of publicizing libraries and their services through professionally produced and distributed radio and television spots. The project was underwritten with Library Services and Construction Act funds; without such support the television aspects of the undertaking could not have been financed. At that time the author was the public relations consultant for one of the participating library systems and was deeply involved in the project. There is no doubt in her mind of the impact of radio and television upon the average listener and viewer.

Although the televised announcements had to be general in character since they represented the offerings of five library systems serving rather diversified populations, people came into libraries throughout the geographic area covered by the stations and remarked with delight, "I saw my library on television!" Actually, in most cases this was not true, but each

An imaginative shot to publicize library-supplied poolside paperbacks.

viewer was thrilled to think that something with which he could identify was appearing on a national network. Sheet music was printed for the jingle accompanying the library commercials and elementary school music teachers had fun orchestrating it or using it for choral groups. A light-hearted gaiety surrounded the presentation, which placed the library in a new psychological setting. It was portrayed as the "in" place to go.

In some instances, radio listeners came into their respective libraries and repeated almost verbatim what the announcement had suggested they ask for. Teenagers listening to all-music stations seemed especially receptive to the announcements related to using the library's resources as a way of staying in school. Some of them mystified librarians by saying, "Sloopy sent me." Sloopy was the lead singer in the rock band version of the library jingle, the librarians learned.

The participants in the program had hoped that New York State would be able to finance the project on a statewide basis or that the American Library Association would make the recordings and video tapes available nationally on an at-cost basis. Unfortunately, neither of these possibilities materialized, although a few scattered states purchased the materials directly from the producer. The empirical evidence gained through the experiment, however, remains to be employed intelligently and professionally at such time as libraries in a given area can agree that reaching new patrons through the mass media is as legitimate an expenditure as any other library budget item.

6

DEVELOPING ADDED CHANNELS
OF COMMUNICATION

One of the simplest of communication channels, which many libraries overlook, is the telephone directory. Too often the library is listed only once under its formal name: Henry V. Newkirk Memorial Library. A patron must feel very frustrated indeed if he cannot remember the library's full title and does not find another listing in the telephone directory under "library" or "public library." Sometimes referring his query to the information operator doesn't help very much because she doesn't know the correct name of the library either and she may or may not have a cross listing provided through the courtesy of the telephone company itself. A municipal library may be listed under "Village of Mountain View." Such a listing is an even worse blunder since remembering the library's name won't do any good. The patron must remember that it is a municipal library as well. Multiple telephone directory listings are not costly and a library has no excuse for not making its telephone number as widely and readily available as possible.

The telephone manners of the library staff are, of course, an integral part of the public relations program. A full appreciation of this may lead the director to reexamine the location of the main telephone for incoming patrons' calls and to reassess the attitude of the personnel assigned to receive the calls. A harassed clerk confronted by a patron refusing to pay her fine and three teenagers indulging in a little horseplay can hardly be condemned for failing to respond graciously to a telephone inquiry. The question is not whether she has failed, but whether she should be placed in a situation where she cannot help failing. The human beings at the desk are much more pressing in their demands than the disembodied voice on the telephone and the clerk will respond accordingly.

Renewals, simple reference questions, inquiries about the time of tonight's program, and similar library business transacted over the telephone should be given equal status with on-the-spot patron service. The caller asking who won the 1927 World Series may be a local barber trying to settle an argument. He may also be the mayor's administrative assistant, trying to settle an argument. The identity of the caller should make absolutely no difference in the type of treatment he receives. If there are extraordinarily busy hours during which the library staff simply cannot handle telephone calls adequately (perhaps when after-school use by students reaches its peak), rather than give short, impatient answers it might be better to have a recorded announcement explaining that the library cannot take incoming calls between 3:30 and 5:30 P.M. because of the great number of patrons in the library, and requesting that the individual call back later for prompt service. Recorded messages on the telephone are so commonplace that an unsatisfactory reaction is unlikely. The message can indicate a secondary number to be called if there is an emergency.

Good telephone manners are especially important in relation to calls made to the library director's office. The laconic reply, "He's not in," is exasperating to the caller. What does that mean? He is down the hall? He has gone to play golf? He is ill? Certainly to reveal that the director is at a meeting and will return at 2:45 is not giving away a state secret. Meanwhile, the secretary should try to ascertain what the caller wants, particularly if he sounds like someone who is in a complaining mood. In such cases it sometimes mollifies the individual if the secretary is permitted to offer to have the director return the call. The disgruntled person feels he has already scored a point and this relieves the tension. The director cannot help but be better prepared to handle a verbal onslaught if he has an idea of what's coming (and has had a brief chance to get some background information from his staff) than if he receives or returns a telephone call completely off guard.

The telephone is being used imaginatively by a number of libraries. Recorded messages greet the patron when the library is closed and invite him to the next library-sponsored program. During the World Series, one library has the correct score inning by inning on the telephone. Another library produces five-minute recorded bedtime stories to which young children can listen over their home telephones. Special dial-a-fact equipment is available for projects such as bond and budget campaigns. The telephone is such an obvious medium of communication that it is frequently overlooked and its full potential as a public relations tool is not developed.

As has been pointed out earlier, no single channel of communication will reach everyone and repetition is required to make the message stick. Less dramatic channels of communication than newspapers, radio, and television exist in almost every community and should be exploited by the library. Many churches have weekly bulletins distributed or mailed to their members. An excellent public relations gesture, for example, would be to request the opportunity to mention Lenten reading materials in these bulletins at the proper time, and to have the appropriate books grouped together at the library for those patrons who are attracted through this medium. Many synagogues maintain libraries on Jewish heritage and culture. Supplementary books on special loan from the library's collection may be the prelude to additional library patronage by interested borrowers.

Civic associations, fraternal and veterans' organizations, and similar smaller groups of individuals provide excellent opportunities for one-to-one contacts on behalf of the library. Such groups have well-defined focal points of interest. The library should be able to zero in on the specific concerns of each group and to offer appropriate materials or services. In one community, the local veterans' organizations were overwhelmed when the director offered them the use of the library parking lot as the staging area for their annual Memorial Day parade. Centrally located, free of cars on a holiday, situated on the main street of town, the parking lot was ideal for this purpose. The veterans had never thought to ask for it, but the library director, seeking new ways to reach groups within her community, hit upon this idea and acted upon it. Subsequently, the veterans made an unrestricted gift to the library, and this custom has continued over the years.

A company of volunteer firemen was deeply appreciative when the local library called their attention to its film on mouth-to-mouth resuscitation. They had been aware that the library stocked films, but not *that* kind of film. This does not mean that each fireman then became an avid reader. It does mean that the library had generated a friendly feeling among these men, that some of them might be less hesitant to enter the library, and that the chances of their Yes vote on the annual budget had been strengthened.

A very perceptive library director capitalized on an inquiry from the local chapter of the Sons of Italy to launch a public relations activity of major dimensions. A member of the group called at the library to inquire what books the director would suggest he purchase to start a small library on Italian culture at the lodge's headquarters. Seizing on this opportunity, the director conducted the visitor out into the main reading room and took him from one area to another, pointing out books on art, music, exploration, physics, literature, poetry — all either by or about Italians. The visitor, amazed at the wealth of material at the library related to Italian contributions to society, expressed the wish that all members of the Sons of Italy might become aware of the library's resources. The director at once invited him to hold one of the monthly meetings of the lodge at the library with the library assuming responsibility for the program. This offer was made in October and it was agreed to hold the program in mid-March. This gave the library five months to get ready, and the staff needed every minute of it.

Objects such as lace, leatherwork, pottery, and characteristic Italian handicrafts, borrowed from private collectors, were placed in the library's exhibit cases. The meeting room was decorated with flags of the various city states of Italy borrowed from the Italian travel bureau. Costumes were borrowed from the Italian cultural attaché and members of the library staff of Italian descent were requested to wear them the night of the program. Recorded music was selected to be played while the guests were arriving. Available motion pictures on Italy were previewed and it was decided to show two: a superb film on Michelangelo and a light, humorous travelogue featuring Venice, a train ride through the Dolomites, and scenes of Italian artisans and craftsmen at work.

Paralleling these activities, the public relations consultant on the library staff conferred with the publicity chairman for the Sons of Italy and the program was mentioned both in the lodge's regular monthly newsletter and in a special invitation sent out by the group. Of course, publicity stories were released to the weekly and daily newspapers. Contact was also made with the ladies' auxiliary chairman for advice on Italian-style refreshments. During these activities the fact emerged that the local chapter was the largest in the United States and, to the members' knowledge, the first lodge to be singled out for special recognition by a public library. The two congressmen representing the area were requested to insert remarks in the *Congressional Record* commending the Sons of Italy for their untiring efforts to project the true image of the Italian-American in the face of undesirable publicity generated by a small segment. The congressmen complied and reprints of their remarks were made available on the night of the program, a major surprise for those in attendance.

The evening was completely successful. There was standing room only for the films. The Italian-style pastries and coffee provided a nice post-program opportunity for the audience to examine the many examples of materials related to Italy which the library had assembled for display in the meeting room. Was this major public relations effort worthwhile? Unquestionably. Since the founding of the library, the section of the community largely inhabited by Italian-Americans had voted No on everything. They did not want a library to begin with. They did not want a building. They did not want a branch. They did not approve the annual budget. But in June after the celebration, the budget vote in that area was Yes, and so it has continued. A plus for all libraries is the fact that the head of the lodge became state chairman and will probably be elected national president of the Sons of Italy. When libraries come up in conversation, he is likely to put in a good word on the national level.

Some communities are dominated by one or two major industries in which a large proportion of the population is employed. Customarily such industrial complexes have a house organ and frequently several internally issued publications. Libraries very seldom make contact with plant employees through this communications channel. Yet information about books on hobbies, planning a vacation, improving one's home, cooking less expensive meals, and many other topics might prove interesting to the readers of a plant's own publications. Editors of house organs are usually seeking material with a fresh slant to fill their columns, and an offer of library news geared to employee interests might prove very welcome. If an enormous plant, such as a major aircraft company, employs so many thousands of people that they come from widely scattered geographic areas, the libraries serving the combined populations might share the chore of supplying copy to the house organs.

Libraries might also offer to make films available for employee lunchtime programs or for entertainment the night of a company dinner. The appearance of news about the public library in the plant magazine or other evidence of the library's interest in the industrial worker may come as a surprise initially.

Continuity along these lines will carry the conviction that the library wants to serve the factory workers as well as their bosses. Many of these men and women, the so-called blue-collar workers whom many libraries have failed to attract as patrons, may feel for the first time that the library has something of genuine value for them.

Persons with impaired vision constitute another group to be reached. Comparatively few library users are adequately acquainted with the extensive collections of large print books now available for all age levels. To publicize these books is important for two reasons. First, the library may regain a former patron whose failing eyesight makes reading normal print an impossibility. If he drifted away before the advent of large print books, how can he have heard about them? Second, families whose older members can no longer read normal print need to know about large print books. It's a good feeling to be able to take a book home to an aged mother who would just love to read if only she could see well enough. Many libraries have used an unfortunate approach in publicizing large print books. Almost all of the flyers, reading lists, and bookmarks the author has seen have been printed in ordinary type. This, needless to say, is self-defeating.

The most obvious communications channel through which to reach the partially sighted is public service radio announcements, but there are other approaches which should be explored. The individual who has failing eyesight is usually in touch with a doctor either in private practice or in clinical work. These professional men will welcome a letter from the library director calling their attention to large print books and enclosing a printed sample showing how large the type actually is. It is especially important to point out that books suitable for children and young adults are included in the collection. The social security agency is another dissemination point for information about large print books. Most of its clients are over sixty-five and seeking ways to enrich their lives at the least possible cost.

A related area is that of talking books. Now that their use has been extended to anyone who cannot turn the pages of an ordinary book, a major effort should be made to publicize their availability. Hospitals, nursing homes, and homes for the aged are especially grateful for information about talking books. One librarian was delighted to find that emotionally disturbed children would listen to a talking book although their behavior was so distracting that "in-person" readers could not complete the story. Whether technically the player and books should have been lent to this center for the emotionally disturbed is a moot question. Certainly the children were unable to handle a book in any accepted fashion. The gratitude of their parents for some small evidence of normality was unbounded. To think of such an outlet for this facility was creative public relations on the part of the librarian responsible for talking books.

There is a great deal of talk about library service to shut-ins and it usually revolves around delivering books and retrieving them. Librarians should inquire whether some of these individuals, who live alone with few friends or visitors, would not prefer talking books. After all, the voice of the reader is a human sound in an empty room.

It is not possible to describe all the communication methods that an ingenious library director and his staff can devise. In addition to those already discussed, it may be possible that the local bank or utility company will include an item about the library along with its monthly statements; in some cases, banks have paid for good-looking bookmarks to be distributed to library patrons and bank customers. The adult education director in the school system may be willing to include a reminder in his course listings that books for required or supplementary reading are available at the public library. (The library might consider grouping some of these books together for patron convenience at least during the early weeks of the semester.) Each library director will have to examine the composition of his community and select those channels of communication likely to be the most productive for his purposes.

So far, all of the discussion has centered on making use of avenues existing outside the library to reach the many segments of the public who should be library patrons. A major channel yet remains to be considered — the library's own publications.

Generally speaking, these fall into three categories: newsletters, giveaways, and reports.

A library newsletter can be a very useful communications tool if it is truly a *news*letter. In too many cases, a newsletter sounds like a good idea and is launched with very little thought about the time and effort involved in editing and circulating such a publication while the contents are still news. Not everyone can write the tight, lively prose which makes for good newsletter copy; a pedestrian, plodding note creeps in or else, in a determined effort at levity, the style and contents become "cute" and dreadful. No library should issue a newsletter unless it can squarely face up to these questions: Why do we need a newsletter? For whom are its contents intended? How often will it be issued? Who will be responsible for amassing the news, writing, editing, and production? What methods of distribution will be used?

The most valid reason for issuing a newsletter is that the director and the trustees feel the library's message must reach the public through a direct channel in addition to the

nonlibrary avenues of communication. The library-issued newsletter has a major advantage over mass media communications
— the library can tell its own story, in its own language, and
release this information at the most propitious time. If the
library is confronted with a hostile newspaper, the need for an
official channel of communication may be acute. Or if the library
has a multifaceted program going on with many new services,
activities, and personnel involved, a newsletter may be the best
way of tying all these items together to present a cohesive picture of what is happening at the library.

A newsletter can be used to editorialize about library
plans or problems in a manner unacceptable in a newspaper release. Special events can be announced much farther in advance
than newspapers are willing to do. The newsletter can give behind-the-scenes views of life at the library which tend to humanize the institution but which are not strictly news items.

An attractive, well-written newsletter can be a valuable public relations tool. Its contents, however, cannot be successfully selected unless it has first been determined to whom
the newsletter is addressed. Some libraries have mistakenly
attempted to devise a newsletter equally satisfactory for internal
and external consumption. This is an impossible combination.
Library personnel presumably know how a book is acquisitioned
and don't want to read about it in the newsletter. Conversely, a
VIP on the mailing list won't waste his time reading social
trivialities about library employees. In most cases, a library big
enough to need an internal newsletter will have a staff association which may be willing to take on this assignment or a full-
time public relations person who can turn out two publications
for two different audiences.

The frequency of issue of the newsletter is another
difficult decision. In the author's opinion, a newsletter should
come out when there is news. In some very active libraries with
a great deal of programming and community involvement, there
may be monthly issues. In other situations, a quarterly publication is sufficient. One library states on the masthead of its newsletter: "Issued from time-to-time." The editors wait until they
have something to say, which is usually four times a year. Once

periodicity has been established, it should be adhered to. A newsletter issued on a hit-or-miss basis fails in its mission of conveying interesting news regularly to a selected readership.

Selecting a good editor for the newsletter and giving that individual released time in which to do the job is another hurdle. While volunteers with professional editorial experience may be satisfactory in some instances, if the library wishes to exercise control over the contents and style of the newsletter, the editor had better be a paid employee (even on a contractual basis specifically for the newsletter). The editor should be completely familiar with the library, a facile writer with a lively style, and possessed of some feeling for layout and appearance. The newsletter should be the mutual responsibility of the director and the editor, exchanging ideas and assessing what is to be included in each issue. The actual writing, proofreading, and supervision of production are the editor's job. Policy decisions are the director's job.

A newsletter can be mimeographed, photo-offset from typed copy, or typeset and printed. The choice of reproduction method is dependent upon the financial resources of the library and the number of copies to be distributed. A newsletter going to 800 people is a likely candidate for the mimeograph machine. A newsletter with a circulation of 17,000 copies should probably be printed. The author can see no point in a newsletter whose circulation is limited to the copies patrons pick up at the library. Presumably they are already acquainted with the library and are the least in need of added information. A basic mailing list, in her opinion, would comprise all elected officials, the presidents of all of the major organizations in the community, officers of the PTA, clergymen, members of the Chamber of Commerce, the board of education, principals of schools and heads of departments, college presidents and librarians, presidents of major corporations, the entire membership of the Friends of the Library, and VIPs in residence (that is, identifiable members of the local power structure), *plus* anyone who indicates to the library that he would like to be on the mailing list. Anyone who takes the trouble to ask to be on the mailing list is certainly entitled to this courtesy. In medium-sized communities with populations

*Book cover giveaway makes inner-city students'
schoolbooks walking advertisements for the
public library.*

of up to fifty or sixty thousand, it should be possible to send a
newsletter to every household, assuming four members to a
family or a circulation of 15,000 copies per issue. Postage and
printing would still be within reason. Beyond that figure, the
specialized list would appear to be the only financially feasible
circulation policy unless some outside organization agrees to
underwrite the newsletter. Over the years the Library Public
Relations Council has given awards for unusually well-edited
and good-looking newsletters. A note to the LPRC president
(the organization is listed in the *Bowker Annual of Library and
Book Trade Information*) can put novices in touch with past
contestants who can provide samples of award-winning newsletters for inspiration and guidance.

     All other forms of library-produced materials, with the
exception of the annual report, the author groups together as
"giveaways." Reading lists, bookmarks, souvenirs of special anni-

versaries, National Library Week items, shopping bags, memo pads, lapel buttons — all of these devices, and many more, she views as valuable mainly in generating a friendly feeling toward the library among those people who are already using it. She has serious doubts that even the most handsomely produced reading list entitled "Southeast Asia in Crisis" or "Crime in the Streets" will actually attract a nonpatron into the library. Such skepticism is probably heresy.

If the library has the manpower and the money, it may be possible to produce reading lists intended for specialized groups within the community. Thus, if the Protestant Council of Churches would like a Lenten reading list for distribution through its member churches, it would be a fine gesture if the library could oblige. In this instance, by means of the particularized approach, a few nonpatrons might be attracted to the library, especially with the added impetus of their church's encouraging them to read during the Lenten season. But such a list, produced for general distribution over the checkout counter without a direct channel to an involved group, will probably reach no more patrons then those already using the library.

One type of giveaway which has proven especially popular is a list of books suggested for Christmas gift-giving. Patrons are grateful for this help at the holiday season. Books should be grouped according to age level and subject matter, with the title first. Prices as well as publishers should be included. This list, however, must be available early in November if it is to be of any value. The patron who is considering giving a book needs help well in advance of his deadline if the book must be ordered from an out-of-town source. In some areas, bookstores and book sections in department stores welcome copies of this list and display the recommended books, thus giving the library's efforts added exposure among nonpatrons.

Certain National Library Week materials can be used effectively with prominent individuals on a one-to-one basis. One library system purchases enough mobiles each year to send one to each elected official, newspaper editor, and major corporation executive in the county. Accompanying the mobile is a personal letter from the local NLW chairman requesting the recipient

to hang the mobile in his office during National Library Week to show his constituents or clients that he is a friend of the public libraries. Sending the mobile by itself would be unproductive. The accompanying letter, reminding a busy individual about the library and its services fifty-two weeks in the year, is the important public relations strategy. Without this annual mobile mailing, the library system would find it difficult to devise a reason for communicating personally with some of these influential people. Thank-you letters have shown that the recipients appreciate, even look forward to, this NLW promotion.

Other items are also effective as giveaways. Patrons like to feel that a "plus" was added to their visit to the library, and a reading list or bookmark provides that plus. The bookmark may also contain some information of lasting value which will incline the patron to keep it — the hours of service, a list of the bookmobile stops, a simplified version of the Dewey Decimal System. Or the bookmark may merely encourage him not to use some less desirable substitute to mark his book. The reading list may be effective in pointing up some aspect of the library's collection unfamiliar to the average patron, and the fact that such books are on hand (even if he doesn't want to borrow any of them) may be a source of pride and satisfaction to him. There is nothing wrong with these goals for reading lists and bookmarks. To retain the library patrons you have is a legitimate reason for producing or purchasing giveaways. To rely upon them to attract additional patrons is a very hollow hope indeed.

The same observation holds true in relation to items like lapel buttons with catchy slogans such as: "I'm a card-carrying library patron." Friends of the Library may enjoy wearing them and they may bring warm smiles to the faces of nonpatrons who don't actually hate the library, but it is very doubtful that such a gimmick will attract the nonpatron to the library. The motivation is too shallow. As it has been previously stated, the library must demonstrate that it can perform a meaningful function — a function related to an activity already meaningful in the life of the nonpatron.

The annual report of a library is a public relations tool of prime importance. It presents an excellent opportunity for the library to sum up its accomplishments and to set forth its plans. In too many cases, the annual report is a compilation of statistics interspersed with a few sententious remarks. If the library can afford professional public relations assistance on only one thing, it should be the annual report.

An annual report to be effective should have a recognizable theme. The report can trace all of the behind-the-scenes operations (and personnel) involved in putting a single book on the shelf. The anecdotal method can be used to illustrate the library's service pattern. Quotations from patrons expressing satisfaction with services can be coupled with explanations of the people, time, and money required for a given service. A typical day in the library can be used to demonstrate the multiplicity of activities involved. One year, children's services can be highlighted; another, services to homeowners; a third year, community outreach. A fresh format should be sought as well, to emphasize fresh contents.

The annual report in a number of instances will also include the budget proposed for the next fiscal year. It may even be a plea for an affirmative vote on the budget. This dual purpose makes it especially important that the report be readable and convincing. Some libraries have found that instead of giving a line-by-line budget analysis, it is more effective to group expenditures under broad categories which any recipient can understand. Thus contracts for window cleaning, minor repairs, custodial supplies, etc., would be grouped under "Housekeeping," while light, heat, power, telephone service, water, etc., would be grouped under "Utilities." Unless one of these categories contains an unusual item which needs special mention (and this can be done in the text), such a summary is all that the average taxpayer requires. Copies of the detailed budget should, of course, be available at the library.

In an annual report, the library should stand on its own merits. Invidious comparisons with neighboring libraries are undesirable and dangerous. Perhaps the following year, the tables will be turned and uncomplimentary circulation or book-stock figures will apply to the library which initiated the comparisons. If the library has genuine accomplishments — more reference questions answered, better programming for young adults, a reading station opened in a housing development — they should be noted. And if there are unsolved problems — dwindling patronage in branches, mutilation of books, difficulty in recruiting qualified personnel — they should be mentioned, too. An institution characterized entirely by sweetness and light sounds "too good to be true" and probably is. The best annual report is one which achieves a delicate balance between eliciting compliments for a job well done and sympathy for problems recognized but yet to be solved.

The annual report should never be allowed to deteriorate into an apologia for the library's shortcomings. Lack of money to do what the library knows it should be doing is a *symptom*, not a cause. If the funds are not forthcoming to accomplish more, the library should be reexamining its pattern of service, its efforts to recruit new patrons and to retain existing patrons. An institution — public or private — which is not progressing is retrogressing. No library can rest on its laurels. They are prickly and perishable.

7

ATTRACTING PATRONS THROUGH
SPECIAL EVENTS AND PROGRAMS

Library literature abounds with examples of special events from ethnic festivals to the staging of pseudo-coffeehouses where all of the furniture was removed from the children's room. Some of these special events have made a suitable contribution to the on-going public relations efforts of the library. Others have subjected the library to ridicule and occasionally to outraged protests, and one wonders who authorized them in the first place. The same rule of thumb applies to a special event as applies to a news story — if it isn't good for the library, it isn't good. A spaghetti-eating contest at the library might result in a lot of publicity and please some smeary-faced participants. Such a desperate and ill-conceived attempt to "humanize" the public library would reveal that the director and his staff have an imperfect concept of the library image they are trying to project into the public consciousness. Even if the biggest spaghetti manufacturer in the country offers to supply the spaghetti, the library should decline with thanks. A library does not endear itself to the community by losing its inherent dignity and self-respect.

Well-conceived special events offer excellent opportunities to encourage members of the community at large, or particular segments of it, to visit the library, see for themselves what kind of place it is, and relinquish some of their prejudices and misconceptions. Let us examine the hypothetical spaghetti-eating contest in the light of this dictum. To whom is the library attempting to appeal? Youngsters? Their parents? Italian-Americans? Will the participants be any better informed about the library or feel any deeper degree of involvement after the event than before it occurred? This type of event is well suited to the recreation program of a school system or the municipal department of parks. It is not suited to a public library because after the hilarity has died down, few people will feel differently about the library than they did before the event.

The exact opposite of this nonproductive type of special event is a series of programs stressing ethnic and racial contributions to the culture of the city sponsored by one of the great metropolitan libraries. Dancers, musicians, poets, and authors of the highest caliber representing the nationalities and races involved have participated in this series of events held in the appropriate neighborhoods. Entire blocks have been roped off for dancing and games typical of the countries being honored. As many as six thousand people have been attracted to a single library branch in a two-day period. No one could leave these festive occasions without feeling that the library cared for him as a human being with a cultural and racial heritage of which both he and the library are proud.

A library birthday party featuring a cake twelve feet in diameter with the mayor himself cutting the first slice will attract a great deal of publicity. It may also attract some individuals in the community who are curiosity-seekers and have nothing else to do that afternoon. It is very doubtful if this event will tell anybody anything new or worthwhile about the library except that it is a year older. Such a birthday event, however, skillfully handled as it was at one public library, can become a significant high spot in the community's activities, talked about for a long time afterward.

Capitalizing on the current interest in astrology, the public relations officer for this library prepared twelve sets of questions and answers, one for each sign of the zodiac. Library patrons who came to the birthday party, which was well publicized in advance, were given a sheet of questions according to their respective birth dates. Twelve areas in the library from the reference section to the children's room were designated by signs of the zodiac and guests were asked to circulate through the library, find their corresponding sign, and then obtain the answers to their questions. The questions involved using the card catalog, the *Readers' Guide*, out-of-state telephone directories, college catalogs, children's books, and many other segments of the library's collection. Some questions required the use of more than one library tool. At each zodiac sign was a librarian to help and encourage the patrons in their search. It was a mad, happy scramble. Patrons enjoyed the game while learning something about their library's resources. The winning patrons received gift certificates for books. The traditional birthday cake followed.

Over five hundred people attended this event, some little girls in party dresses because they had been invited to the library's birthday party. Patrons even requested copies of the questions they had not been assigned to answer just for the fun of ferreting out the information. This type of special event, requiring careful advance planning and an intelligent recognition of what the library is hoping to accomplish, is the only kind to which the author can give her endorsement.

A special event is a tricky affair because so many variables are involved: the weather, the adequacy of advance publicity, unanticipated competing events or catastrophes, the willingness of the library personnel to give their wholehearted cooperation. Two factors, more than all others, appear to make for a successful event: detailed advance planning and the existence of a "core group" whose attendance can be counted upon.

Special events do not occur in a vacuum. They should emerge from a recognized need of the library to reach a well-defined group who are not using the library or who — in the case of the astrological birthday party — are faithful library patrons for whom a pleasant afternoon's diversion is warranted. One astute library director, realizing that a good many No votes on the library budget emanated from the Irish-American section of his community, agreed with the public relations specialist to hold a three-day Irish festival. This Irish-American group lived the furthest distance from the library and because of the geography of the community, had the least satisfactory access roads leading to the library. For this group, a visit to the library was a major undertaking. Quite a few had never been through the front door. The intent of the festival was to encourage nonusers to come to the library and thus to dispel their preconceptions that the library was far removed from their daily lives.

Three events were planned which it was felt would involve all age levels — an exhibition of Irish step-dancing, an Irish fashion show with models drawn from the high school population, and a Sunday afternoon showing of films about Ireland paralleled by a story hour and a "littlest leprechaun" contest for small children. About six months of intensive planning were required for the events which took place, of course, over the St. Patrick's Day weekend.

Arrangements for the fashion show were made through Irish International Airlines (Aer Lingus), which supplied all of the clothing as well as a commentator with a suitably soft brogue to describe the garments. The fashion editors of the daily papers were alerted to the event in advance since the clothing to be worn on Saturday would leave Ireland by air only the previous Thursday. The home economics teacher at the high school assisted in selecting the teen-age models, and the PTA Council supplied the names of several of its members who could model the more sophisticated adult clothing. Whole groups of the community — Irish or not — became involved in the fashion show. Mothers wanted to see their daughters as models and friends wanted to see their teenage peers. Seating was limited and the demand for free tickets was very high.

While the programming was unfolding, the public relations specialist was in touch with the Irish Linen Guild;
Waterford Glass, Inc.; china shops carrying Belleek; and spe-
cialty shops selling Irish dancing shoes, shillelaghs, sheet music,
and other novelties. The display cases in the library, filled with
such borrowed items, provided an excellent background for advance publicity pictures. The meeting room of the library was
decorated with travel posters, photographs of Ireland, and historical items such as handbills advertising the Abbey Theatre.

The Irish American Society was asked for the names
of its members in the library's area. A special invitation to the
festival was sent to them. The civic associations and churches
in the area were alerted. Attractive folders were prepared for
widespread community distribution inviting everyone to attend
(since "there's a little bit of Irish in us all.") Posters were
strategically placed in stores, schools, banks, churches, and other
appropriate spots. Advance publicity appeared in the weekly

newspaper and the two dailies. An upward spiral of excitement and interest was generated.

Over a thousand people attended the three events — all of which had limited seating capacity. Older members of the Irish-American community were especially appreciative of the appearance of the step-dancers, who reminded them of their own youthful days. There were requests for a rerunning of the films on Ireland, some with the explanation "so I can bring the grand-children." Travel posters which appealed nostalgically to attendees were removed from the walls and given away at the end of the festival. Items donated by the Irish Linen Guild were used as door prizes. Amazement and delight were expressed that the library should have gone to so much trouble "just for the Irish." It was a totally successful special event because it fulfilled the criteria which should govern such an occasion: it attracted a new group of people to the library, offered them something meaningfully related to their lives, and left them with a feeling of warm goodwill.

Some libraries may feel that such an event is far too expensive for them to contemplate. A careful check of expenditures shows that the Irish-American festival cost approximately $150 or 15 cents per person. This is a very modest investment to attract potential support for a library whose annual operating budget has crossed the half-million-dollar mark.

A routine event taking place at the library because its meeting-room facilities are available for public purposes sometimes can be turned into a special event with skillful suggestions from the director or the public relations officer. At one library, the United Nations Association was planning a rather ordinary observance of the twenty-fifth anniversary of the United Nations. The library director and the public relations officer, however, suggested to the chairman and her committee that members of the Association be asked to wear some garment, hat, piece of jewelry, or other accessory typical of a foreign country. The response to this idea was excellent since many individuals in the community owned authentic costumes either inherited or purchased while traveling. Immediately, a gala atmosphere began to characterize the event. The committee decided that perhaps a buffet supper featuring international dishes could take place preceding the program and made suitable arrangements, with the library's consent. Next, the school system, hearing of the advance planning (which began in June for the following October) decided to hold a poster contest with a United Nations theme and asked if the prizes could be awarded the evening of the celebration. The library offered to display all of the posters submitted and to supply the prizes (the silver medals issued in honor of the UN's twenty-fifth anniversary). Finally, some internationally flavored entertainment was provided by two professional folk singers who volunteered their musical talents.

What had started out as a rather uninspired evening of listening to a speaker from the United Nations, who might have attracted 50 people, turned into a community event for which the 150 available tickets at $5.50 each (to pay for the buffet supper), were snapped up immediately. The library had endeared itself to the United Nations Association and it had also provided both the setting and the know-how to spark an important community event. The public relations overtones of such a joint effort are even better than those generated by a special event sponsored solely by the library.

To summarize: (1) a special event is valid only if it attracts a new segment of the population to the library or rewards a faithful group of patrons; (2) it should have a well-defined purpose and should be directed toward a core group whose attendance is fairly well assured; (3) it requires from three to six months of detailed planning and cannot be carried out successfully without cooperation from top to bottom among the library personnel involved; (4) it is a legitimate expense for a library since it may provide a significant channel through which to reach an indifferent or semi-hostile group upon whose goodwill the financial future of the library may depend.

Many libraries today have the facilities and the budgeted funds to offer programs on a variety of topics. Programs are not the same as a special event, which is a onetime, all-out effort with a single focus. Programs should be looked upon as a regular, continuing offering of the library for the enjoyment and enlightenment of patrons. The hope, of course, is always that the

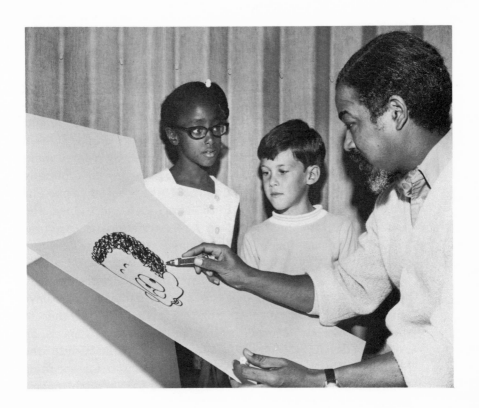

subject matter will attract newcomers to the library; but even if this objective is not achieved, the importance of good, well-selected programs is not vitiated. Here, again, the library should be concerned with added inducements for keeping its present patrons in a happy frame of mind.

Programs can include everything from a lecture series to showings of classic movies, from cartoon drawing to book review luncheons. The scope of programming will be dictated by two factors: the readiness of the community to attend library-sponsored programs and the staff time available to plan and carry out programs. Some communities are so overorganized, so "meeting happy" that almost anything the library can afford to offer in the way of programs will meet with little response. Such a community is the one mentioned in connection with the United Nations celebration, a special event which aroused a high degree of active interest. In this same community, a lecture on modern art drew eleven people. Film showings of motion picture classics have been discontinued because of poor attendance. Not more than fifty people came to hear the author of a widely-read book on the touch-me sensitivity movement. Obviously for some libraries, series of programs are a misuse of staff time, which might better be devoted to other aspects of public relations.

In another community characterized by a large number of retired people, library programs have proved especially popular. They are free. The library is in the heart of town. The subject matter has been chosen to attract men and women who want to "keep in touch" but can no longer afford the lectures and entertainments they once attended. This library has had standing room only for its motion picture classics, and adults have been willing to sit on the floor for a lecture series on ESP, psychic phenomena, graphology, and yoga. Some libraries have found the film buffs in their area eager to band together to sponsor showings of experimental, off-beat films. This is an excellent device to attract avant-garde individuals into the library. It also shields the library from criticism for spending public funds on what the more conservative patron might regard as questionable films.

In the author's experience, film programs for the general public are more successful when a theme ties the selections together. Publicity for the series can be more cohesive and appropriate tie-ins of displays or exhibits can frequently be devised. It is also desirable for the film showings to be on the same night of the week and the same week of the month. "Watch for the Wonderful Wednesdays!" has become a slogan in one community to remind patrons of the once-a-month motion picture series. Themes which have proved successful are Academy Award winners (but the library must be sure to get the *original* version of the film — there's a great deal of difference in the drawing power of the Ronald Colman version of *Lost Horizon* and a subsequent remake); films made during the Irving Thalberg era at MGM; Kings of Comedy; Days of Glamour (Marlene Dietrich, Carole Lombard, Myrna Loy); Best of the Bad Guys (*Frankenstein, Little Caesar, Public Enemy*); and of course, a Greta Garbo festival.

Sometimes it is fun to launch a film series with a small-scale special event. Thus, in one library, on the first night of the old-time movies, the staff wore straw hats, striped vests, and sleeve garters. Penny candy (courtesy of the Friends of the Library) was sold in the lobby. Recordings of the music used to accompany silent films can be obtained from the Museum of Modern Art in New York City to provide an appropriate overture for the evening as patrons are arriving.

Film showings seem unusually popular with young adults down to the junior high school age. The library may want to consider two showings — one in the afternoon for the younger children who may prove somewhat disruptive, and one in the evening restricted to high school students and adults. A word of warning: experiments with the showing of silent films, including such classics as *The Hunchback of Notre Dame,* with Lon Chaney, have not been successful. It takes a real aficionado to sit through a silent film with no accompanying mood music. Somehow, risibility sets in and pathos vanishes. This comment is based on comparatively limited observation and is open to question. A library may want to try one silent film before making a decision pro or con.

Increasingly popular and less time-consuming than a grandiose book-and-author luncheon are box lunches at the library during which a qualified individual reviews a book related to his field of expertise. Thus, the psychiatrist at the county hospital reviews *In Cold Blood,* and the local college president reviews *The Greening of America.* Usually the guest reviewer will decline any fee or ask only for his expenses if travel is involved. For a very sophisticated audience, a "name" reviewer may be indicated. A careful screening of likely prospects frequently turns up someone eager to ride his hobby if given the chance. A prominent columnist who is outspoken on environmental topics may welcome the opportunity to sound off on a particular book on conservation. He may waive his customary fee entirely. The best approach is to ask the individual whom you want, having in mind the top fee the library can afford. If he declines or names a price far above your maximum, all that has been lost is a telephone call. And more often than not, the VIP (surprised and flattered at being invited to do something at a library), will accept the invitation.

Usually in this kind of programming, the only fee charged the patron is the cost of the box lunch. The program costs are paid for out of library funds. Since a box lunch probably will not cost more than $2.00, book-review sessions put this type of literary event well within the means of the average family. Tickets for book-and-author luncheons at major restaurants are so expensive in many areas that interested patrons cannot afford to attend. If the Friends of the Library are willing to underwrite a book-and-author luncheon, the library may want to consider one. Otherwise, the smaller library-centered event seems to generate much goodwill and to leave attendees with a feeling of having spent a worthwhile lunch hour at the library. Businessmen are sometimes able to attend during the noon to 1:30 P.M. time slot and this programming opens up a new avenue for reaching the men in the community.

Some libraries have become involved in concert series, community theatre productions, and similar programs which must be offered off the premises. The author has very serious misgivings about the validity of this type of commitment. To her sense, the basic purpose of programming is to attract people to the library who would not otherwise come or who, as regular patrons, deserve a "plus" for their patronage. If the program is held in the local high school or the community theatre, how many people in the audience really acknowledge that this is a library-sponsored event? As far as enhancing the library's image is concerned, the program might just as well be sponsored by the Knights of Columbus or B'nai B'rith.

If the library has no meeting room or is so overcrowded that on-premise programs are impossible, it is time for the director and the trustees to be making plans for expansion. *Temporary* use of other quarters might be justified in this case to retain the goodwill engendered by programming in the past. To begin a program series away from the library, and to continue it elsewhere when adequate physical facilities for something less ambitious are available at the library, appear to the author to generate only the most marginal form of goodwill.

Programming for teenagers presents a problem area in many libraries. While the author cannot endorse a simulated

BEFORE: Young Adult Review Boards organized fundraising book fairs in Missouri with widespread radio and TV cooperation.

AFTER: Proceeds were transformed into 8mm cartridge film loops for everyone's enjoyment.

coffeehouse with an all-night "rap session" going on, neither is she so sanguine as to expect that young people will be attracted to the library by the same types of programs which interest adults. Lectures have to be on "hot" topics. Today, it's yoga and astrology. Tomorrow it may be Buddhism and health foods. The criteria in planning a young adult program must be whether an interest has been expressed in the subject matter *ahead of time.* Generally speaking, young people do not want to attend a program which is going to inform them. If the program is going to entertain them and at the same time increase their information about a topic in which they are already interested, the library may find it has planned a successful evening.

Karate and yoga demonstrations and talks on the history of jazz, on electronic music, on ESP, on how to get along with one's parents are among the programs which have proved successful to the author's knowledge. Book discussion groups appeal to a relatively limited but vital segment of young people if the books under discussion are focused on a topic relevant to today's youth. Thus, youthful perspective can be gained on the generation gap through readings which reveal the centuries-old nature of the problem as well as its current manifestations.

Some libraries have a young people's advisory council which works with the library officer responsible for young adult programming to offer suggestions and assist with publicity. Such a group has excellent public relations potentials if the library is genuinely willing to listen to what the young people have to say and to act upon their advice if at all possible. Young people everywhere are cynically disillusioned with adults who solicit their opinions and then ignore them. For such a group to function successfully, ground rules should be laid down in the beginning governing such factors as how much money can be spent and what types of programs will be completely unacceptable. The basic purpose of the library in sponsoring programs should not be violated for any age group. Within this framework, a teenage advisory council can probably come up with some extraordinarily good program ideas.

As its own contribution to bridging the generation gap, the library may want to schedule one or two family-style evenings each year which fall somewhere between programming and special events. Topics such as skiing, skin diving, camping, and vacation planning offer a drawing power which spans the generations. Coupling motion pictures on skiing with a display of the latest in skiing gear turns an evening program into a mini special event. Converting the parking lot into a weekend exposition of campers, trailers, and equipment for outdoor living makes a special event out of a continuous showing of movies on the national parks. Often parents welcome such programs during winter and spring vacation periods when the college-age members of the family are at home and it is difficult to find an activity of interest to everyone.

Good programs are like the bonus glassware offered by the local gasoline station. If you are a regular patron, the glassware is a nice "plus." If you are not a patron, you may stop by just for the glassware and discover that this is a very friendly service station you would like to patronize regularly.

8

DISPLAYS AND EXHIBITS AS A PUBLIC RELATIONS TOOL

Window displays serve two purposes. They provide the merchant with a showcase for his wares and they entice the passerby into the store for a possible purchase. In much the same way, displays and exhibits at a public library can provide a showcase for aspects of the library's collection and they can attract possible patrons into the library building. To the author, a *display* is a collection (large or small) of related items or of items related to a theme which is assembled in one of the glass-enclosed cases commonly found in libraries. An *exhibit*, in her terminology, is a showing of paintings, sculpture, photography, or similar works of art in the meeting room or gallery area of a public library. While the choice of terms may be arbitrary, the words will be employed in this context in this chapter. It is not the author's intent to deal with bulletin-board displays, which are covered in depth in Mona Garvey's comprehensive book *Library Displays: Their Purpose, Construction and Use.*

The first hope of any public relations officer who is responsible for creating attractive displays is that the cases in the library are "workable." In many instances the physical limitations imposed by the cases themselves are so severe that to install a handsome, eye-catching display seems almost impossible. If the library is planning a new building or if renovations are in progress, it would be ideal for the public relations officer and any staff members involved with displays to have the opportunity to present their ideas on the subject. For example, the case should not be more than 18 inches deep nor less than 12 inches. Objects are lost when too far removed from the viewers, while an excessively shallow case prevents the use of a large book or even an article such as a handsome tray or bowl of large diameter. The floor of the case should be 30 inches from the floor level of the room. A practical interior height is 48 inches. A single section in a bank of display cases should probably be not wider than 72 inches.

There are two types of display-case doors — sliding glass panels and glass panels in hinged frames. Both have their disadvantages. Sliding panels can usually be locked with a small, relatively inconspicuous serrated metal tongue over which a specially designed padlock slides and grips the serrations when the key is removed. This form of closure leaves the viewing area unencumbered and the case presents a single unbroken visual impression. The hinged panels, of course, have a frame and when two of them are swung together and locked, a sharp vertical element effectively bisects the display, destroying some measure of its artistic unity.

In terms of installing a display, the hinged doors are preferable since they open fully and permit the worker to reach in both directions to position whatever is being shown. The sliding doors, on the other hand, overlap each other so that the display worker is constantly having to shift the doors from side to side to reach first the right and then the left area of the case.

An ideal arrangement would be sliding glass panels which recess into the walls *on either side of the display case* when the exhibit is being installed. If this is not feasible, the hinged doors are a more workable solution, since with practice the display artist can compensate for a dividing line which he knows will exist when the doors are closed.

The shelves should be easily movable with supporting brackets that can be adjusted at varying heights. There should be an assortment of shelves of varying lengths to provide for diversity in the display instead of shelves which (as is customary) stretch uncompromisingly from one side to the other and give the installer no opportunity for creative groupings or for introducing visual dynamics. In addition to the standard plate-glass shelves, the library might purchase a second set made of handsomely grained wood.

The walls and back of the case should be lined with a fine-textured corkboard or substance of similar composition which readily accepts tacks, pushpins, staples, and straight pins. The author has not found pegboard a suitable lining for display cases. The available fixtures for pegboard display purposes are limited and have little flexibility. The pegboard surface resists tacking and pinning. If it is covered with fabric, wallpaper, maps, Currier & Ives prints, or any other material to provide a decorative background for the display, removal of the covering usually results in unsightly damage to the pegboard and to the covering material. In libraries where pegboard backing has already been installed in the display cases, covering the walls with carpeting is an excellent solution. If the library has monochromatic or tweedlike carpeting, the cases can echo the decorative color scheme of the main reading room.

Display cases should have internal illumination, preferably tubular *incandescent* lighting, located at the top and bottom of the case. Fluorescent lighting may be injurious to old books, manuscripts, and delicate colors in fabrics; this risk should be taken into consideration when displays are installed in cases with fluorescent lighting. It is desirable to have an electrical outlet in each case so that small motor-driven objects, tiny electric fans, and spotlights may be installed when appropriate to enhance displays.

Discovering suitable displays for the library is a major undertaking and multifaceted from the public relations point of view. First, there should be a policy governing the use of the display cases. Are they to be confined strictly to materials selected and arranged by the library staff? Are community groups to be permitted to use them (Red Cross, Girl Scouts, Hadassah)? If so, under what circumstances may a community group install an exhibit? How long may it remain? Are there any stipulations as to the appearance and content? Do displays originating with the library take precedence over local organizations? (For example, if National Library Week and the spring drive for community concert subscriptions conflict, is the display policy clear in order to avoid wounded feelings?) Some libraries have fallen into the habit of relinquishing their display cases to community organizations by default. Lacking energy, manpower, or imagination to locate and install their own displays, these libraries have contented themselves with "letting George do it," and generally speaking, George does a pretty poor job. By taking this laissez-faire attitude, the library is passing up an excellent opportunity to reach people within its community who have something exciting to display. It is also neglecting an important launching pad for newspaper publicity.

Second, displays should be scheduled at least six months in advance. A last minute assemblage of hastily obtained objects will never produce the impact of a display whose contents have been selected with care and with a *thematic* approach. This type of planning, backstopped with a fully understood library policy, should obviate any conflicts with community groups wishing to use the display cases. To be absolutely honest, the author has serious reservations about the public relations value of displays installed by local groups. They are pleased with the results, but is anyone else? Possibly to ingratiate the library with a sizable group in the community (especially if there are a number of display cases to be filled), such a privilege should be extended for limited periods of time. The privilege should remain a privilege, granted anew each year upon application, and not by repetition allowed to be mistaken for a right. The contents of the library's display cases should be viewed as part of the total public relations program and not simply as items to fill an empty space.

Displays in shop windows, on counters in stores, in the aisles at supermarkets have become increasingly sophisticated and artistic since many of them are supplied to local merchants by the advertising agencies handling the particular products included. The library cannot afford to have its displays of the crepe-paper variety if it hopes to compete for public attention in the marketplace of ideas. The *thematic* approach to a display gives it cohesiveness and also provides a publicity angle for news releases. For example, the public relations officer in one library heard about a retired missionary whose hobby was collecting shoes from all of the places in which he had been stationed during his career. She visited his home, made selections from his collection (which proved to be very extensive), and had the shoes installed in two cases four feet high and eight feet long in the lobby of a library. The shoes included a Manchurian actor's boot with platform sole, a shoe for a Chinese woman with bound feet, sandals made of lion's hide with the fur still on, delicately embroidered satin slippers for harem favorites, intricately carved clogs, and many other examples of unusual footgear. The theme of the display was "How Does It Feel to Stand in Another Man's Shoes?" The library issued a reading list of books on brotherhood and international goodwill, thereby deepening the significance of the question. Excellent publicity was accorded to the display and patrons actually stood in line to view the cases. The public immediately recognized the fact that this was museum-level material.

Two points in the preceding account need to be clarified. First, it is absolutely necessary to see a collection before agreeing to display it. A telephone message from a patron that she owns a collection of milk glass sounds very promising. A visit to her home may reveal that her entire collection consists of reproductions, which can be purchased from Williamsburg, Virginia, to Sturbridge, Massachusetts. To retreat tactfully from this situation is not easy. Certainly an on-the-spot rejection would be disastrous. Usually a reference to the fact that the library plans its displays six months in advance (a wise procedure) and that the public relations officer will be in touch with the patron about the possibility of a future display will end the visit courteously. A follow-up letter thanking the patron for her offer and saying that the library will be in touch with her "if it is possible to include your collection in our schedule as it develops," should conclude the entire matter without too much loss of face on either side.

The second necessity is an insurance policy to cover objects while on display and while being transported to and from the library. Such a floater policy is not unduly expensive and its existence can be a source of reassurance to an individual who would like to lend his collection of paperweights but is concerned about security. In most instances, knowing that the display cases are locked and usually located in areas under surveillance while the library is open, collectors feel relatively free to cooperate with a library. This does not relieve the library of the responsibility to provide adequate insurance coverage in the event of damage or theft. In all of her years of obtaining and arranging displays, the author has known only one object to be broken. As it happened, the owner had his own insurance policy and refused reimbursement. Nevertheless, a library should have insurance coverage which stipulates a total value for the collection plus a maximum value for any single item displayed.

It takes an inquisitive turn of mind to locate first-rate displays. Talking to the owner of a wholesale paper warehouse one day, the author noticed a small silver elephant fall from his pocket. Jokingly she asked him whether it was his good luck charm or an evidence of his political affiliation. He explained that collecting elephants was his hobby. Immediately, she asked him whether he would consider displaying his collection at a nearby library. The man refused on the grounds that he had had one bad experience in lending part of the collection to a public school where it had been mishandled. She then suggested that he stop in at the library, see the quality of objects on display, and perhaps reconsider his refusal. Six months later the collector telephoned her to say that since other individuals had lent such precious objects as a collection of antique bells, he would like to offer his elephants. Could she come to his home and make a selection? Expecting fifty to sixty elephants to choose from, the author found over six hundred, ranging in size from a bracelet charm to the base for a coffee table. Examples from this collection in ivory, silver, wood, jade, crystal, Lalique glass, and other precious substances, as well as elephants in the form of candlesticks, vases, teething rings, bottles, dagger covers, and similar oddities filled two very large display cases and attracted many people to the library.

Human-interest stories in newspapers often provide a clue to a collector who will be responsive to the opportunity for a public display of his collection. Old-fashioned campaign buttons (thousands of them), salt and pepper shakers (hundreds of them), decoupage (used to illustrate a book on the subject) are among the items uncovered through a simple telephone call saying, "I read about your collection in the newspaper. Would you be interested in displaying it at the public library?" So few people think of the library as a possible showcase for their prized possessions that a negative answer is rarely received. Even if the collector refuses, he is flattered by the request.

Museums sometimes are excellent sources of display materials since many of them have warehouses full of items which lack of space precludes exhibiting. Long-range planning in this instance is absolutely essential. Museums move very slowly and through channels so that a six months' headway is not too long. Moreover, a museum usually lacks staff time to plan a display. The objects will be loaned, but it is up to the public relations officer of the library to decide upon the theme and to ask the museum for the kinds of articles to be included. "In the Good Old Wintertime" might be an appropriate January theme. The library can ask for such articles as sleigh bells, old-fashioned ice skates, footwarmers, beaver hats, bonnets, a buffalo skin robe.

"Visions of Sugarplums" might be a Christmas theme with antique dolls, quaint games for children, doll furniture, even a doll house if the case will accommodate it. The natural history museum may be willing to lend stuffed birds from its collection which can be displayed as "The Hunter and the Hunted" — birds of prey and their quarry. The direct channels through which the local museum or historical society can obtain publicity are limited, and this added opportunity to place its wares (and by implication its need for more space) before the public is often welcome. Larger museums, of course, may have packaged displays available to both schools and libraries. While these are good space fillers, they lack the unique quality of a display assembled solely for the library.

There are commercial sources of displays — trade associations, major insurance companies, greeting card companies, travel bureaus, banking institutions, manufacturers of business machines and computers — a lengthy list. Sometimes what they have to offer is most appropriate. On other occasions,

the author has found that the material arrived from a previous
exhibitor in poor condition or was inappropriate for the space
available in the particular library for which it was intended. A
concise description of what is to be expected, how it is to arrive,
what its next destination is to be, and other pertinent data
should be obtained before the library commits itself to use such
displays. Disappointments and misunderstandings can thus be
avoided. (The manager of a shopping mall in the Midwest wrote
the author inquiring why she had shipped him an enormous
wooden crate with a padlock for which he had no combination.
He had no record of ever requesting her to send him anything.
The crate contained framed medieval manuscripts lent by a
greeting card company with instructions to ship them to the
shopping mall, which would receive the padlock combination
directly from the card company. It took several long-distance
telephone calls to set matters straight.)

Whether books should or should not be included in displays is a debatable question. Some libraries object to removing books from circulation during the period of the display. The author feels that books related to a display, if not actually inside the case, should be on a nearby book truck or rack to encourage patrons to extend their use of library resources. The tie-in does not have to be on a direct basis (after all, the reading list for the footgear exhibit previously mentioned was not about *shoes*), but related reading materials can be offered. Antique dolls can certainly be accompanied by books on how to collect them; they can also be flanked by books such as *Hitty: Her First Hundred Years*. Similarly, the display of salt shakers, "Add a Pinch of Salt," was related to books on gourmet cooking.

What, then, is the purpose of worthwhile, well-planned displays in a public library? First, displays dress up the place. Just as guests are pleased when it is evident that their hostess has looked forward to their coming and has made preparations accordingly, so displays in a library give patrons the feeling that an effort has been made to make their visit more enjoyable. Repeatedly, the author and her staff when installing displays have had complete strangers stop and thank them for their efforts with such comments as: "They add a great deal to my library visit," and "I sent my husband in last week to look at the coin collection." Libraries need this friendly aura to help dispel their false tomblike image built up over the years and still lingering in many minds.

Next, the displays, especially if drawn from local sources, encourage nonpatrons to come into the library. When it is known that Jack's collection of Civil War memorabilia is on display at the library, it is fairly certain that his relatives, some friends, some members of his church, his lodge, his Legion post will stop in to look at it. If these individuals are already library patrons, added goodwill is generated by the fact that their friend has been singled out for recognition. If they are not library patrons, they may be encouraged to look around and perhaps borrow a book since they are on the premises anyway.

Lastly, displays provide a "peg" on which to hang publicity about the library. Encouraged by a well-written news release, the newspapers may decide to interview the collector. They may dispatch a photographer (what a great shot of a little kid looking an angry stuffed osprey in the eye!). The library itself may have photographs taken for distribution to the newspapers. It may even turn out that the collector is sufficiently knowledgeable and articulate to present a library-sponsored program on his hobby for a special-interest group in the community. When followed up, a murmured comment by one library trustee — "My wife has some nice lace she could display" — resulted in three display cases full of exquisite and rare specimens and two lectures by "my wife," who was discovered to be an authority on crocheted lace and a consultant to museums. The publicity was gratifying to everyone involved.

The author has chosen to define *exhibits* as "a showing of paintings, sculpture, photography, or similar works of art in the meeting room or gallery area of the library." The purpose of these exhibits is identical with that of displays: to create an inviting image for the library; to attract people to the library building; to provide a springboard for publicity. The problems, however, are somewhat different.

An art exhibit involves the element of taste, whereas a display is usually not open to question on aesthetic grounds. Why someone should want to collect four hundred candlesticks may be open to question, but it is highly unlikely that his collection will offend anyone's aesthetic sensibilities. This is not true when it comes to painting, sculpture, photography, and the other visual arts. Words like *good* and *bad*, *like* and *dislike* come into play and their implications for public relations cannot be ignored by the library sponsoring the exhibit.

When a continuing series of gallery exhibits is to be held, the library would do well to follow one of two courses: select an individual of some stature in the art field and place him in charge of the gallery or else organize a committee of knowledgeable citizens to screen potential exhibit materials. The library cannot dissociate itself from what is hung in its gallery. If there should be repercussions about the content of a particular exhibit, the director and the trustees will be fortified by having the unbiased judgment of a qualified professional or a well-chosen committee to rely upon. There is no implication of artistic censorship in this suggestion. The question of whether a nude is too nude for a library art gallery should not be left up to the personal preferences of the library staff or the trustees. Acceptability should be based on qualified professional judgment and not on any other criteria. When such objective judgment supports an exhibit, adverse reactions are likely to be nonexistent or at an acceptable minimum.

The art director or citizens' committee performs another valuable function. Once it is known that the library is exhibiting artists' works, a veritable parade of people will arrive lugging with them canvases, statues, and photographs. Some will be real "finds" and others so lacking in talent as to be embarrassing. The time of the director should not be occupied in seeing these would-be exhibitors nor should he be placed in the position of making the final decision on the artistic merits of their work. Rejection via impersonal screening is easier to accept than rejection by a library director whose qualifications the artist may feel are not very impressive.

Some libraries, aware of the public relations implications of rejecting marginal exhibitors, have an annual "Sunday painters" show in which anyone in the community can exhibit an example of his work. Such shows can sometimes be held out of doors and combined with music or folk dancing to provide a festive atmosphere. Another approach is to have an annual "juried" show to which every painter may submit pieces he feels are worthy of inclusion. Those selected feel honored; and since only the jury knows who was rejected, the unsuccessful artist can console himself with anonymity. Occasionally a group show can be assembled with examples from a number of artists, none of whom has sufficient works of merit to fill the gallery but each of whom has several really good pieces worthy of exhibition.

Occasionally the question arises whether the library's gallery should not be reserved as a showcase for local talent in the interests of good public relations. The author's answer is a resounding No. Just as a library should feel no obligation to display a milk glass collection composed of reproductions which anyone can buy, so the library should not feel obligated to lower its standards of artistic merit merely to provide a local artist with an opportunity for a one-man show. While the library is not the cultural arbiter for its community, it should adhere to recognized standards in any area where aesthetics are involved.

Works of art, of course, present an insurance problem somewhat akin to that of displays, but more serious in nature. There is no point in having an exhibition if the gallery is kept locked and patrons are admitted upon request only. The possibility of theft or mutilation exists in a library as it does in any public gallery where an artist displays his works. The artist must agree in advance to the maximum insurance coverage the library carries for the entire exhibit and to the maximum value which can be placed on any piece in the exhibit. Of course, if a painting is damaged, the insurance company will step in to determine a reasonable market value for the piece. The painter cannot arbitrarily set a figure representing what the painting is worth to him. Over the years the author has known of only three examples of damage in exhibited items — a mustache drawn on a photograph, a piece of statuary accidentally knocked from its pedestal, and a cigarette burn on a wall hanging. In each case, the artist was not nearly so disturbed by the episode as the library personnel.

Naturally, both the artist and the library want to derive as much publicity from the exhibit as possible. It must be understood from the beginning that the library has final control over how and where the exhibit will be publicized. The artist is a temporary tenant in the library and as such must abide by the regulations set up by the landlord. Patterns of operation vary but generally speaking, if the artist wishes to hold an opening, the library stipulates that he must pay the bill for any refreshments (no alcoholic beverages) and for any additional custodial help. Openings are frequently held on Sundays since most libraries (unfortunately) are closed that day and this gives the artist some control over the people who will arrive to view his show and eat his food. Many libraries, by keeping guest-books, have assembled mailing lists of community residents who enjoy art shows and should be invited to openings. To a library list an artist will want to add names of people important to him. If he is not from the local area (and a sizable library will soon attract exhibitors from considerable distances), the library public relations officer will want to work with the artist to be sure that newspaper critics and VIPs from the library's community are on the guest list.

The format of the invitation and its content are usually the responsibility of the artist. He may design it and the library may supervise the production, or he may handle the invitation from start to finish. Under any circumstances, the library should always see a final version before it goes to press. If the artist pays the bill for the invitation, the library reimburses him for the added copies needed to cover its own mailing list. In many cases the mailing piece can be designed to serve both as an invitation and as a catalog/leaflet for the exhibit. Library patrons will pick up such leaflets in quantity, and a workable solution is for the library to purchase the multipurpose leaflets and then to bill the artist for whatever number he needs for his own use. Some libraries prefer not to quote prices in the catalog/leaflet. They will, however, either give a patron the artist's address and telephone number or will keep a price list at the circulation desk to answer inquiries.

Photographs are essential in publicizing an art exhibit. If the artist does not already have some good quality 8 x 10 glossies of his work, the library should arrange for such photographs to be taken. Those that are used by the library are paid for by the library, and the artist pays for any additional prints he may want for his personal use. An important point needs to be made here: although the art show appears to benefit the individual artist, the fact that it is located at the library is beneficial to the library. From this viewpoint, it is legitimate for the library to invest some of its own funds in an art exhibition exactly as it would in a program or a special event. The library pays a fair share of the cost of an art exhibit because it is going to take a fair share of the credit for sponsoring such a valuable contribution to the cultural life of the community.

If a library is shorthanded, art exhibitions, in the author's opinion, should have a low priority among the public relations chores to be accomplished. Deftly handled, with a certain flair, they provide an excellent form of enrichment. But unless sufficient personnel are available to work closely with the artist and to shepherd each show through its opening and publicity, other forms of outreach are likely to pay higher dividends for the effort invested.

9

STRUCTURING AND WINNING
BOND AND BUDGET ISSUES

The most sophisticated campaign ever devised for a library bond or budget referendum cannot succeed unless it is based upon a sound foundation of good public relations stretching back over a number of years. As was pointed out in the opening chapter, shoddy goods cannot be disguised for long with fancy wrappings. Someone is going to peek inside. Actually, the test of a library's public relations efforts comes in some communities every year when the annual budget vote occurs. In other instances, where the library is a line in the municipal budget, the amount of public opinion which can be brought to bear on the city government to insure adequate support for the library may accurately reflect the image the library has created for itself in the public mind. When a library has outgrown its quarters or when funds are needed for a major renovation or an overhaul of services, the willingness of the public to approve a bond issue or an increase in the millage rate will usually tell the story of how successful the library has been in achieving a meaningful place in the life of the average citizen.

A library which is faithfully serving its community, making an honest effort to retain, recruit, and regain patrons, should have little to fear when it presents its annual budget, even in times of economic recession. If the library has been doing its job properly, patrons know that they are getting their money's worth. In an economically middle-class and below-middle-class community known to the author, the library tax rate is the second highest in the county. A typical homeowner pays about $35.00 per year in library taxes, as do the thousands of families living in the housing development homes. The library budget has risen annually, tripling in the fifteen years since the library was founded. In this short period, heavy library use necessitated a sizable expansion of the original building, a move readily approved by the community.

This is a good library. The board of trustees is representative of the community as a whole and has had a number of changes in its makeup. The director and the assistant director know the patrons and are recognized by them. The clerks at the desk act like human beings. The reference department extends itself to meet patrons' needs. There is an energetic public relations officer who plans special events, displays, programs, exhibits, and film showings, and who publicizes them skillfully. The library issues a monthly calendar of events and a quarterly newsletter. There is a library bus which circuits the community after school and on Saturdays to provide free transportation for children and young adults since the area is bisected by a main highway. There is a bookmobile serving outlying areas in the winter, playgrounds and swimming pools in the summer.

Part of the addition to the original building, which was very open in plan, is an "absolute quiet room," reserved for adults and serious-minded students, thus meeting a very pressing patron need. Viewing the existing building from the user's standpoint, the director and his staff realized that very few people entered through the front doors because the parking lot is in the rear. Needing additional space for the paperback collection, they decided to block off the front doors and use the lobby for book racks. No one is disturbed by this "violation" of the architect's original plan, which was no longer functional. When it became apparent that thefts of books had risen to an unconscionable level, the library installed a turnstile checkout system *with much advance publicity*, explaining that every other method had been tried to no avail. While the turnstile may make users unhappy, at least everyone understands why it was installed and that it is in no way a reflection on the honesty of the average library patron.

The book collection is good — broad and deep — and the periodical collection is the best of any public library in the county. Scattered about the floor in trough-like stands are small groupings of books on timely topics. There is a rental collection for impatient best-seller readers and a seven-day loan collection of other books in popular demand. The library offers conducted tours to any group of three or four people who stop in and ask how to get the most out of their library. An energetic, "with it" feeling permeates the whole building and is reflected in the attitude of those who work there. This library is alive — it belongs — and the community it serves so creatively has supported it accordingly.

How different is such a library from another known to the author where the library director forbade an adult patron to charge out a book because she knew that previously the woman's little boy had been refused permission to borrow the book (a harmless story) on the grounds that he did not hold an adult card. "You are simply trying to circumvent the library's regulations," this director announced, "and I do not intend to permit it!" That this library is one of the most ill-supported in the entire area is hardly a matter for surprise.

Assuming that the library has already laid a good groundwork through a well-conceived and conscientiously carried-out public relations program, certain techniques are effective in telling the story and in getting out the vote. Since a bond issue is usually even more difficult to interpret than a budget, the author will use the former as an example; but all of the activities described (slightly modified) apply equally well to an intensive budget campaign.

Fundamental to a successful campaign is unanimity on the part of the board of trustees and an energetic, devoted director. If the board is not unanimously committed to the bond issue, the dissidents must either agree to support the majority in the democratic manner or else resign from the board so that they can conduct their offensive openly and not from ambush. In one community where the board of trustees was divided four to one on a bond issue, at every public meeting the minority member arranged for someone to stand up in the audience and say, "Mr. Johnson, speaking not as a member of the board, but as a private citizen, how do you feel about the bond issue?" Mr. Johnson then proceeded to answer and of course, in the public mind, his answer could not be divorced from his membership on the library board. Presumably he was privy to all of the deliberations which had preceded the decision to submit the referendum to the community and he was still unconvinced. Why? What were the others concealing? This was a devastating tactic and one which contributed in good measure to the defeat of the bond issue. Subsequently the other trustees asked him to resign, an action which should have been taken before the fact, not after it. At the very least, he would not have been able to attend the campaign planning sessions and thus be a pipeline back to the opposition.

The director needs to be prepared to work harder than he ever has before. He should not be expected to sell the bond issue to the community. That is not his role. Actually, he would be suspect if he accepted this role because the assumption might well be that he wants a larger library because he is an empire builder. The function of the director is as a resource person, a behind-the-scenes coordinator, a fact-finder. Even working with an experienced public relations officer, the director must make the final decisions about action to be taken in many instances. His trustees will look to him for a level of leadership and acumen such as they have never previously demanded.

Trustees encumbered by a director who has, for example, already adopted a retirement philosophy at the end of many years of service, will do well to wait another few years till he is gone before tackling a building project. In one extreme instance, the need for a building was so acute and the director so apathetic that the trustees were able to negotiate an early retirement and then proceed with their plans.

The director also has the right to demand loyalty on the part of his staff members *while they are in the library*. A library employee has no right to respond negatively to the query of a patron regarding the bond issue when that employee is on duty in the library. Such conduct amounts to the same tactics used by the dissident trustee described above. The employee has a perfect right to differ with the policy decision of the Board of Trustees and the director and to act accordingly *outside the library*. (An employee, for example, may be genuinely distressed over the location chosen for the new building.) Inside the library building, however, where the policy of the administration must take precedence over personal feelings, the employee should not be permitted to talk down the bond referendum. He should answer questions factually, offering no opinions or comments with emotional overtones. He does not have to volunteer any personal views on the subject. In the case of older, more obstinate employees, the director may have a difficult problem on his hands if serious opposition to the building program develops within his own ranks. Where good internal public relations have been developed, this is most unlikely.

Over a period of time, the trustees and the director should lead the community gently but firmly forward toward the recognition that a new library building is needed. (For simplicity, the author uses the term *new building* generically to cover the original building when a library is founded, major renovations and additions, a replacement for the old building, and the construction of a branch.) A serious defect in many bond issue campaigns is lack of preparation. The trustees tend to present the community with an accomplished fact — a library package that is to be bought although its contents have not been market-tested before the purchaser is asked to pay the bill.

Almost everyone is aware that market testing and opinion sampling are commonplace in the field of commerce and industry. Why should the library feel that it exists apart from the mainstream of public opinion and needs only to unveil its product to win acceptance? The trustees may want first to call in an experienced library consultant to analyze their present situation (they know how bad it is, but let an authority confirm their views) and to present them with a written report which can be released to the community. Paralleling this, it is good practice to appoint a citizens' advisory committee to examine in depth the findings of the consultant and to meet him for discussion.

This process can be reversed. The advisory committee can look over the library's setup, come up with its own conclusions, and then have them verified by an outside expert. In either case, the vital thing is to involve important members of the power structure of the community in the decision that the library needs a new building. The *need* should be fully established before plans to meet the need are formulated. The board should be very sure that it will give a fair-minded hearing to what the advisory committee has to say. Compromises may be necessary or even a rethinking of the board's position. Such a committee should be appointed only if it will be permitted to make a genuine contribution to policy making.

Occasionally a board of trustees, overanxious to be fair-minded, appoints someone to the advisory committee who is an outspoken critic of the library and has been for years. Such an appointment is pure foolishness. Although the individual might be thought of as representing the negative attitudes which will need to be combatted, these attitudes can be defined and coped with later in the campaign, if indeed the trustees and director do not already suspect what they will be. There is no profit in including a confirmed dissident on the advisory committee. He will remain intransigent and will hinder the deliberations of the committee. A well-run bond issue campaign closely resembles a political campaign even if library trustees are reluctant to admit this fact, and no astute politician would invite a member of the opposition to sit in on his tactical planning sessions.

A second defect in many campaigns is lack of time. Although the campaign activities themselves should be compressed into approximately eight weeks of hard work, the preparatory softening-up process may begin two to three years before the date of the vote. Presumably the director and the trustees are aware of deteriorating conditions in the library — lack of shelving, poor ventilation, inadequate lighting, high noise level. A library does not become overcrowded and unsatisfactory overnight. When the physical situation starts to deteriorate, *then* the bond issue campaign should begin. How is this possible? By priming the children's librarian to say apologetically to disappointed parents, "Oh, if we had a new building, we could accommodate so many more children for story hours." By having the reference librarian explain, "We can no longer keep back issues of newspapers readily available because we have run out of shelf space. They are now stored in the basement." By continuing to sponsor adult programs even though the meeting room has been converted to a reading room to handle the overflow of young adult patrons. Let the adults sit on folding chairs in the children's room. They will soon begin to ask themselves, "Was this library always as uncomfortable as this?" (But there should be absolutely no attempt to make the situation appear worse than it actually is.) Continue to maintain as high a level of service as possible with as comprehensive a collection as it is feasible to house in the existing building. Simply tell the truth when patrons complain about the curtailment of services or the inadequacies of physical facilities.

If a Friends of the Library group exists, it may be willing to organize a Saturday morning bus tour of neighboring libraries of recent construction. A conducted tour behind the scenes in the existing building is sometimes an effective way of highlighting lack of storage space, inadequate staff work rooms, dampness, termites, and other unpleasant but unseen structural problems. One library was "blessed" by having its pipes freeze *twice* in the weeks just before the vote.

When the architect is chosen, his credentials should be well publicized in the local press. (It is desirable to invite a representative of the citizens' advisory committee to the board

Genuinely crowded conditions tell their own story pictorially.

meetings at which architects are interviewed if several firms are being considered.) The findings of the building consultant, of course, should already have been publicized along with the recommendations of the citizens' advisory committee. Since both of these reports will probably be fairly lengthy, it is a good tactic to prepare condensed versions to be mailed to all community organizations with a request that they be circulated among the executive board members of each organization. It should be announced in the newspapers that the complete texts may be borrowed from the library. Probably only one person in a thousand will want to read the reports, but the 999 others will not be able to say that they were denied the opportunity.

The public library is a public institution, supported by public funds, and it cannot justify secret decisions relating to such a major issue as a building campaign. This does not imply that the trustees should hold open meetings when they are discussing which pieces of property to buy since such information, revealed prematurely, would certainly not be in the public interest. It does imply that once decisions are firm, the community should be promptly and completely informed.

The author has found that a four-part campaign tends to be the most successful. Part one involves speaking engagements before as many local organizations as possible. The second part involves at least one major public meeting to which the entire community is invited. A series of good-looking informative mailing pieces and giveaways forms the third part. The final part is a concentrated effort to get out the vote.

At least four months before the vote, letters should go out to every community organization — civic, fraternal, religious, social, and political — requesting the opportunity for a representative of the library to speak for ten minutes at a general membership meeting, or if that is not possible, before the executive board. A reply postal card should be enclosed. When two weeks have elapsed, a member of the library staff should make follow-up telephone calls to any organizations which have not replied, explaining that the speaking schedule is being firmed up and the library does not wish inadvertently to exclude them. This will round up a few stragglers and no one can say that a friendly overture was not made to his organization. On the off-chance that a new group has been formed in the community with which the library is unacquainted, a newspaper story should be released telling of this plan and soliciting speaking engagements. Letters of confirmation should be sent to each organization which has booked a speaker.

The speakers should be drawn primarily from the board of trustees. It must be reiterated that the library director should not be used for this purpose. His job is to run the library, keep his staff composed, and answer telephone inquiries and in-the-library questions about the building program, as well as coordinate the campaign. Presumably the trustees represent the community. They, too, are taxpayers and the fact that a new building will cost them money and will add to the civic responsibilities for which they are not recompensed tips the scales in their favor when they speak. Naturally, the board members have lives to lead outside the library and supplementary speakers must be recruited who can assist with this project. A library task force should be organized of about twenty dedicated individuals, each of whom is willing to speak three or four times during the two months preceding the campaign. These individuals may be recruited from the citizens' advisory committee, the Friends of the Library, long-term library patrons, or any other source which will provide a working group as broadly representative of the community as possible. The task force is not the same as the Friends of the Library; they have their own role. It is not the same as the citizens' advisory committee, whose role has really been played by the time the campaign gets underway. The individuals who constitute the task force are, rather, short-term "ambassadors" for the library.

The most desirable setup is a team approach with one trustee and one ambassador assigned to each speaking engagement. It is peculiarly impressive to have an ordinary citizen endorse what the library trustee has said and to add a few intelligent observations of his own. The library staff member who is coordinating the speaking engagements should, of course, look over the list of potential speakers and assign them according to any personal interests which mesh with those of a given organization. Certainly a former commander of the American Legion should speak to his own post and a member of the Dorcas Society should speak to her church.

Briefing sessions will have to be held to familiarize the task force with as many facts and as much background as possible. If the team approach is used, the trustee will be in possession of most of the factual information and the ambassador can fill in with appropriate comments. If the ambassador is on his own, he should have a simple speech, couched in his own terms, and a fact sheet containing basic information (cost per square foot, total shelving, anticipated tax rate, etc.) to which he can easily refer when answering questions. If neither the ambassador nor the trustee can answer a question, he should frankly say so, ask for the questioner's name and telephone number, and offer to obtain the answer. There is no disgrace in not being able to answer a question. To give an incorrect or evasive answer is not only disgraceful, it is dangerous. After the meeting, however, a member of the library staff should telephone the questioner and supply the desired information.

If the organization indicates that it favors the building proposal and asks what it can do to support it, the speaker should request that the membership pass a resolution endorsing the bond issue. When members of an executive board comprise the audience (and they are usually the opinion makers for the organization anyway), their motion can make it clear that it is the executive board taking a position and not the entire organization. Such endorsements are very helpful late in the campaign if the going gets rough. They can be used in a last-minute mailing or in newspaper advertisements.

Some speakers like to take the floorplans with them, as well as a rendering in color of the exterior of the building. Other individuals prefer to show slides. A few people are uncomfortable if they have to bring along any props. Insofar as possible, each individual should present a basic body of information and then tailor the balance of his remarks to the interests of his audience. The speaker addressing the Retired Men's Club will not stress the same facets of library service as the ambassador who is talking to the PTA Council. The whole point of speaking to organizations throughout the community is to convince them that the library will be able to satisfy everyone with its diverse resources and improved services, once it is better housed, stocked, and staffed.

Boards of trustees should be careful to avoid two pitfalls. First, never tell the community that the new library will cost "only 4.5 cents per $100 of assessed valuation." This is only a half-truth which will come back to haunt the trustees when the new building is occupied and operational costs climb. The trustees should frankly state and restate that the *construction* cost rate will be 4.5 cents and that as nearly as can be determined, the operational costs for the new building will add another 8 cents to the tax rate. Such figures will not defeat the bond issue if they come from the trustees. Nobody really thinks a building three times the size of an existing structure can be heated, lighted, insured, and maintained, let alone staffed and stocked, for the same price as the old building. The projected operational cost figure will be harmful to the campaign only if it is released *following* questions from the opposition. If the trustees are straightforward about this fact from the beginning, they have nothing to fear.

The second pitfall is fighting the campaign on the opposition's terms. Every bond issue campaign is going to encounter opposition. Often the board and the director can speculate very shrewdly about the nature of the opposition. Sometimes it comes as a complete surprise. The job of the trustees is to sell the merits of the building program, not to overcome the claims of the opposition. This is not a contradiction in terms. The most devastating opposition is one which is able to divert the attention of the community to a side issue and to prevent the focus from remaining on the merits of the main issue. Thus, one community found itself embroiled in a controversy over whether the new library should be air-conditioned ("My own home isn't air-conditioned.") The opposition wasn't really concerned at all with air-conditioning. This was a clever ploy to undermine community confidence in the economies which had been exercised in planning the building. Each time the issue came up at a public meeting, the trustees answered it calmly, pointing out the reasons for air-conditioning and reiterating that the real issue was not air-conditioning but whether or not the library should move out of a horribly overcrowded storefront location. In other words, the board members constantly shifted the focus back to the real issue: Do we or don't we want a good public library — a library of which this community can be proud? They won.

In the heat of the campaign, the temptation is very great to try to convince everyone of the rightness of the library's cause. That task is impossible. In every community there will be staunch supporters of the library. There will also be avowed enemies. Between the extremes is the majority of the population, some individuals well-disposed, some ill-disposed toward the library. The entire thrust of a campaign is to shift enough of the middle group over to the plus side to achieve a victory. Do not waste your time or break your heart over entrenched No voters. You cannot budge them off their base. Leave them to heaven and zero in on those uncommitted individuals whom you may be able to influence affirmatively.

None of the foregoing should be construed to mean that the opposition can be ignored. Where there are legitimate answers, they should be given. In one campaign, six days before the vote, the weekly newspaper carried an apparently well-reasoned, even-tempered letter from a resident who compared the square-foot costs of the proposed building very unfavorably with those of two newly-built libraries in the immediate area. The letter writer claimed that he was in favor of a new library but not at such an extravagant cost. (Trustees should learn to close their ears to sentences which begin, "I'm in favor of the library but . . .") The library, fortunately, had prepared for possible last-minute opposition and now that it emerged, the plan was put into operation. In anticipation of such a need, 6 x 9 postal cards on mimeograph card stock had been imprinted on one side with the library's address and postal indicia. Gummed labels for every resident in the community had already been typed. It was only a matter of deciding what to mimeograph on the postal cards, applying the labels, and getting the cards to the post office within twenty-four hours.

The director and the public relations consultant decided that the best plan was to *agree* that comparative cost figures are very reliable and then to point out that such cost figures have to be updated in order to make the comparison valid. With the aid of their architect, they were able to determine how long ago the bids had been opened on the two nearby libraries. Extrapolation of the applicable cost-per-square-foot figures over the many months that had intervened during which building costs had risen approximately 1 percent per month proved that the letter writer's figures were completely reliable. One of the new libraries would have cost $44.40 per square foot at current construction rates, the other $46.00. The proposed library building was pegged at $45.00 per square foot, right in the middle between these two figures.

Late in the afternoon, by the time the president and vice president of the trustees were able to reach the library, a suggested postal card message had been prepared and was subsequently approved. No mention was made of the letter in the newspaper. (Not everyone reads the local weekly and a library should take great care not to publicize its opponents' claims.) Rather, the postal card indicated that the trustees were taking this opportunity to clarify a point which had arisen and which they were glad to be able to answer satisfactorily. The letter writer later congratulated the trustees on the passage of the referendum but put them on notice that he would keep his eye on them in the future. The feeling was mutual.

While the trustees are telling the library story out in the community, a convincingly written, attractively designed mailing piece should be prepared by a knowledgeable person. Literature for a building campaign (like the annual report) is a type of publication for which it is wise to consider employing an experienced professional in the public relations field unless the library has such a person on its staff. Two pieces of literature are a minimum, in the author's opinion. The first should be a comprehensive brochure which includes the proposed program in detail, the reasons for its timeliness, the background for the board's decision, reproductions of the floor plans and the exterior rendering of the building, construction costs, and the estimated tax increase.

Such a mailing piece needs to skirt the hairline between being handsome and being "flossy." Competing with the avalanche of junk mail received by the average homeowner, the mailing piece has to have sufficient eye-appeal to attract attention. The library should not make the mistake of assuming that anything it mails out will be read just because it is from the library. The informational brochure must stand on its own merits. An overzealous public relations consultant should beware, however, of producing something so striking in appearance and so apparently costly that the recipient becomes concerned with the question "Who paid for this?" rather than with the message the brochure contains. Viewing the types of printed materials other libraries have produced in connection with a building campaign may provide practical guidelines. Frequently the winner of a John Cotton Dana Public Relations Award is a library which has conducted an outstanding bond-issue campaign. The winning scrapbooks can be borrowed on interlibrary loan from the American Library Association.

The second mailing piece should be a reminder postal card received not more than two days before the vote. People are forgetful. The library is not the most important thing in their lives. They need a last-minute reminder. The design of the postal card may repeat some element contained in the initial mailing piece, thus providing visual continuity. The message need not be from the library. It can be from the Friends of the Library, from the library task force, from the presidents of the organizations which have endorsed the bond issue. Since the decorative side of the postal card can be printed in advance, the decision as to what to include on the obverse can be postponed until very close to the mailing date if — and this is a big *if* — the library has a very reliable addressing service or has sufficient manpower to handle the mailing internally. In order to insure its carefully timed arrival, the postal card will probably have to be mailed first class. (The initial brochure, however, should go out on a bulk mailing permit.)

All kinds of supplementary mailings and reminders are possible if manpower and money permit. One library sent a mailing to everyone who had attended a program in the two years prior to the vote, reminding him of how much more enjoyable these events might be if they could be held in a comfortably furnished, properly ventilated meeting room. The Friends of the Library can send a special mailing to the group's entire membership. Bookmarks can be inserted in outgoing books at the circulation desk. Displays or posters related to the building program can be installed in the windows of appropriate stores. Campaign buttons can be distributed. Flyers can be prepared for distribution at the railroad station the day of the vote if the businessmen in town are largely commuters. The list is limited only by the ingenuity of those who are involved in the campaign, available funds, and manpower.

While the initial mailing piece is being prepared, preparations should also be moving forward for at least one open public meeting to which the entire community is invited through a notice in the initial brochure and newspaper publicity. The meeting (or meetings if the community is unusually large or if its geography necessitates more than one meeting) should include remarks by the trustees, corroborative statements by the library consultant if he can attend, acknowledgment of the work of the advisory committee, and an illustrated presentation about the building by the architect, who *must* attend. The president of the board of trustees may chair the meeting. In some communities, however, where feeling is running high, it may be advisable to ask an impartial individual, respected in the area, to moderate; an organization such as the League of Women Voters can often provide a skillful chairman. All questions should be directed to the chairman, who can field them to the board member or other individual best qualified to respond. The fraction of a minute which it takes the chairman to designate the respondent gives everyone on the platform a chance to regroup his mental powers and be prepared. Furthermore, opposition members in the audience tend to rise and shake fingers (or even fists) at the president of the board, but if he is seated at a table as part of a panel, the gesture loses its menace. An impartial chairman seems to "cool it" all around.

Many trustees have felt it well worthwhile to hold a dress rehearsal of the main public meeting. It is valuable to have someone at this rehearsal who acts the part of the devil's advocate and asks all of the ugly and impossible questions likely to arise at the meeting. The trustees accustom themselves to replying and are much more poised when the questions are asked at the meeting itself. Since the author has often played this devilish part, she can attest to the peculiar smile which crosses the face of a trustee as he responds with composure to a tricky question for which a rehearsal has prepared him.

The telephone is the most effective instrument in getting out the vote and plans should be made in advance for installing telephones either at the library itself, a neighboring bank, the civil defense office, the American Legion Hall — any relatively comfortable place — which can be used throughout the day of the vote. Telephoning is tied in directly with poll watching. There is no point in reminding someone to vote when he already has voted.

Prior to the vote, duplicate sets of cards should have been prepared. These cards represent the names of all of the registered voters in the community. If registration is not required, the names of all known library patrons can be substituted or the name of everyone obliged to pay some form of local tax. A fairly comprehensive list of local citizens is a necessity. One set of the cards goes to the polling place with the poll watchers, who can usually be recruited from the League of Women Voters, the American Association of University Women, the Women's Club, or similar organizations. Periodically, runners deliver to the telephone headquarters cards representing the names of people who have already voted. These names are removed at once from the master set of cards on which telephone numbers have previously been written. If one member of a family votes, the cards for the entire family are removed. Presumably if one person has remembered, the whole family will remember. Previous to the day of the vote, the cards of all known members of the opposition have been removed from this master file; no one is obliged to remind them to go to the polls. As for dues-paying Friends of the Library, their cards should have been marked with red checks.

The telephone squad should be the responsibility of the Friends of the Library. The squad member dials a number, introduces herself by name and requests the individual on the other end to vote in favor of the library. There will be some flak. It is too late now to try to sell the building program. All the telephoner can do is to say something conciliatory like, "Oh, I am so sorry that you feel that way," let the critic have his say, and bid him goodbye. No attempt should be made to convince anyone to vote Yes at the last minute. Precious time needed to reach the potential Yes voters is lost arguing with a member of the opposition. As the day wears on, the telephone squad should concentrate on the red-checked cards which indicate the Friends of the Library. During the evening hours, it is especially effective if the callers can be men. There is something quite convincing about a businessman who identifies himself on the telephone and asks for an affirmative vote. Presumably he is hard-headed and economy-minded, yet he is for the library.

When it's all over, thank every volunteer with a personalized letter. (The author assumes that your library will have won. Using the techniques outlined above, she has experienced only one defeat and that was when the effort to get out the vote broke down completely — the opposition, of course, never forgets to come out and vote.) Be generous toward those who despitefully used you and persecuted you. It should be the sincere desire of the trustees and the director to develop a new library of such broad sympathies that it will neutralize all hard feelings and eventually bless the entire community, just as the campaign literature promised it would.

10

FRIENDS OF THE LIBRARY: KEEPING AN ASSET FROM BECOMING A LIABILITY

The title of a delightful book by Joan Walsh Anglund succinctly states, "A friend is someone who likes you." Technically speaking, then, anyone who likes the public library is one of its friends. In practice, however, Friends of the Library when capitalized represents a specific group of people who have paid dues to join a formal organization whose purpose is to support the public library financially and morally. Such a group may be the result of spontaneous generation when someone suggests that a Friends of the Library society be formed and it is. The group may arise through the organizing efforts of the library itself in its formative years or during a crisis period. The Friends may be a genuine working group, vital to the existence of the library or it may have deteriorated into a organization which no longer pursues the original goals for which it was formed. The membership of the Friends of the Library may be composed of energetic, dedicated people without whose efforts the library could not function. It may also be a self-perpetuating "in" group who view themselves as the community conscience in matters concerning the library, but whose faith is without works.

The question is: How to keep an asset from turning into a liability? Experience has shown that Friends groups become troublesome and difficult to deal with when their functions have been inadequately defined or when there is no longer anything meaningful for them to do. It takes a very strong director with a good deal of savoir faire to handle the Friends skillfully once the pioneer period or the crisis days are over. A library should not be hasty to organize a Friends group unless it has a clear-cut idea of what the group can do once the most obvious needs have been met.

This poses a serious problem for the director who may have an inherited Friends association or to whom sincere people may come, offering to organize a Friends group. Any group calling itself Friends of the Library should have a constitution and by-laws which clearly set forth its functions. This document should make it unmistakably plain that the Friends operate in conjunction with the Library, not parallel to it. Any director who fails to make this relationship plain to the Friends at the outset is likely to find himself saddled with a second board of trustees. One community became dreadfully embroiled when the Friends group decided to run its own candidate for the library board — a very questionable action in the eyes of the author. The average resident could not distinguish between someone sponsored by the Friends of the Library and someone whom the library trustees themselves might be endorsing. When the non-Friends candidate won, it was widely presumed that his presence on the board of trustees would be unwelcome since he wasn't the library's choice. Certainly this individual took up his board responsibilities under very inauspicious circumstances. Such impossible situations would not arise if the functions of the Friends were adequately spelled out in the first place. There should never be an implication that the Friends are the "good guys" and that anyone who does not belong to their organization or share their viewpoint is per se a "bad guy."

The Friends function *on behalf of* the library but not *as* the library. This is a fine distinction. The Friends can appear en masse at a meeting of the city council *on behalf of* the library. They are not the policy makers for the library and cannot commit the library to any course of action, become spokesmen for the library, or openly advocate a position which the board of trustees does not favor. These are hard lines. What is to be done when a library has been going downhill or has an indifferent director and an apathetic board of trustees? How can the Friends rescue the library?

The Friends can encourage good people to run for the board of trustees. This is not the same as waging a campaign for a candidate chosen by the Friends. They can confer with the present board and director to ascertain whether lack of money, insufficient professionally qualified personnel, a tired-out administrator, a run-down physical plant, or some other problem appears to be at the root of the downhill slide. As the citizens of the community peculiarly concerned with the library, the Friends can focus attention on its problems and begin to arouse the general public to the need for improved library service. This action may be coupled with an offer by the Friends to pay the fee for a library consultant who will analyze the situation and make specific recommendations for short- and long-term improvements. The Friends can organize "look and see" visits to neighboring libraries for VIPs. They can attend budget meetings and advocate better support for the library — speaking as taxpayers themselves. The function of the Friends is to introduce the leavening element which will cause fermentation in the minds of the board, the director, and the community. It is not to think or act as surrogates for the board.

In one situation in which the library trustees had taken every legitimate step to persuade the village board to schedule a bond issue referendum for a desperately needed new building and had met with utter indifference, the Friends underwrote the cost of a postal card poll of the entire community. The results clearly indicated that the residents wanted a new building. Still unmoved, the village board refused to schedule the vote. The Friends then paid the fee of a renowned library consultant whose report confirmed the position of the board of trustees and provided excellent newspaper publicity. When the village board still continued to look the other way, the Friends paid the fee to have plans drawn up for a new building — money which the library could not have expended without village authorization. This final action turned the trick. A referendum was scheduled (in the depth of winter, on a holiday weekend) which hard work on everybody's part turned into a victory. The softening-up process had taken between three and four years. It is at this point that many Friends groups break down. They want to see immediate results for their efforts — instant success — and if they lack the stamina for the long pull, the group falls apart.

The particular Friends group discussed above was characterized by a broad base of financial support derived from a well-to-do community where many families could easily afford to send a ten-dollar check for their membership dues instead of the stipulated dollar. The Friends board is composed of twelve people, a working number, who meet regularly *with the director of the library*. Through their annual membership drive, the Friends raised the money, made it available to the library to further a building program, and then let the library trustees choose the appropriate consultants. Their support of the library was provided in a manner conforming to the library's purpose. This is the simplest, most direct, and most satisfactory manner in which a Friends group can function. They receive full credit for their generosity and they provide the wherewithal for a library to undertake activities it could not otherwise finance. They do not interfere with or infringe upon the rights or responsibilities of the library board.

Friends can make funds available for programs which the library could not otherwise afford — addresses by good speakers, high-rental films, performances by major musical or theatrical groups. The policies related to underwriting programs need to be carefully spelled out. The library should select the programs, not the Friends. The decisions can be made in conference with a Friends committee, but the library must retain the ultimate authority relative to programs offered under its aegis. This may sound arbitrary. The fact nevertheless remains that if there are repercussions from an ill-chosen program, the library will suffer directly, the Friends only tangentially.

Friends groups also finance library newsletters, leaving the content and the editing to the library administration. Some Friends groups have their own newsletters and of course the library can exercise very little control over their content. If the newsletter is addressed solely to the Friends of the Library, it may be worthwhile to ask the Friends to examine its purpose. A newsletter paid for by the Friends and circulated from the library to the entire community should be productive of far more good-will than one whose circulation is limited to people who are already friendly toward the library.

Another legitimate project for the Friends is paying the bill for the library's annual report and the fee of a professional to write and produce it. The Friends may even be willing to pay for a year-round public relations officer for the library, at least on a part-time basis. Here again, the guidelines must be clearly drawn. The public relations officer is responsible to the director and ultimately to the trustees in exactly the same fashion as any other employee of the library. The Friends are financing such an addition to the library staff because they want to provide professional services to assist the library in its public relations efforts. The individual may receive suggestions from the Friends, may even report to their executive board from time to time, but he must function as part of the library staff.

In many communities, of course, the Friends were the original organizers of the library. They went through all the pangs of bringing it into being, staffed it as volunteers in the early days, campaigned for an adequate building, packed and unpacked the books when a move was made to larger quarters, even sanded and repainted the furniture in some instances. To such people, the lack of "action projects" is very trying indeed. They are willing to raise money, but they also want to perform some service. A smaller library may continue to need volunteers to man the circulation desk, shelve books, conduct story hours, interfile the new entries in the card catalog. The director in such a library has no problem when he is asked by an energetic, determined Friend, "What can I do?" In larger, more sophisticated libraries, the question is not so easy to answer and that is where trouble may set in. The Friends become restless and dissatisfied with their current role. They feel resentful at being cast off by the library. They begin to devise their own projects and to revolve in an orbit of their own. A director must take a firm stand with such a group while using imagination to suggest activities which are not mere busywork but will make a valid contribution to the welfare of the library. Under skillful direction, these restless, energetic people can be used for community outreach projects for which the library has neither time nor manpower.

A Friends of the Library society in a particularly livewire community has organized a birthday project in cooperation with the local Head Start nursery school. The school notifies the Friends as each child becomes four years old, and the Friends present the youngster with a few simple gifts, as well as a beautiful picture book. Frequently this is the first book the child has ever owned. Sometimes it is the only hard-cover book of merit in his home. In some ways this is a small gesture and yet, in terms of human relations, it is impossible to assess its impact. The attitude of the child's family toward the library may be improved when he brings home a handsome book and says, "A lady from the library gave it to me." Perhaps the mother or father may feel encouraged to visit the library and borrow more books for the child. A trail leading to the library has been marked out.

Friends of the Library have been willing to visit beauty parlors, barber shops, bowling alleys, bars and grills, and other gathering places to inquire whether the owners would permit them to install a small collection of books in a specially-built rack to be used for ready reference. The *World Almanac*, a compendium of information about sports, a dictionary, a paper-covered single-volume encyclopedia, and a small assortment of popular paperbacks comprise the collection. The paperbacks may be borrowed without being charged out in any way. Borrowers are invited to return them to the library and pick up something else equally good. Periodically the Friends visit these spots to replenish the collection and to gather information about the usefulness of what has been deposited. One library using this method of outreach made the front page of a major daily newspaper with a picture story about a bar whose patrons were now more interested in reading books than in watching television. The bartender has set up a special corner for books (he has supplemented the library's offerings with some items of his own choosing) and refers to himself as the librarian.

Service to shut-ins is a natural assignment for Friends groups. As previously mentioned, such service may now include large-print books or talking books as well as ordinary reading material. Some Friends have engaged in soliciting donations of best sellers from book club members (who wants to reread most best sellers anyway?). These books are then taken to the local county hospital where they supplement the stock available to patients from the hospital's own resources. Similarly, paperbacks may be collected by Friends to stock book racks at the community swimming pool.

There is hardly a county agency from the children's shelter to the jail which cannot use well-chosen secondhand books (this does not mean either Bobbsey Twins books or "My Adventures Among the Kwakiutl Indians"). If the Friends undertake such outreach projects, however, continuity must be assured. It is unfair to the library's public image for services to begin with a burst of enthusiasm and then die through lack of follow-through. Too often the Friends assume that if they initiate a good work, the library will somehow find the personnel to carry it forward. Genuine activities for Friends should be of a kind which the library cannot undertake without their help and which will not continue if the Friends withdraw their support. This puts it squarely up to the Friends either to fulfill their commitment or to stop making idle gestures.

There remains another category of activities for the Friends: sponsoring special events such as book-and-author luncheons or major outdoor art shows. Unless the director is absolutely convinced, however, that the Friends will manage the undertaking from start to finish, he should refuse to give his consent to such a project. The library cannot afford to have a public fiasco on its hands. Therefore, if the Friends group should fall by the wayside, the library would be forced to throw its own personnel into the breach to save the situation. This is disruptive to everyone concerned. Library personnel resent being asked to pick up the pieces. The public resents the dislocations at the library as professionals are diverted to nonlibrary tasks. The director might have to devote his energies to the salvage operation at exactly the moment when his entire attention should be focused on preparing a budget presentation. Unless the Friends are an experienced, reliable group, some of whose members have been responsible for successful special events arranged for other organizations, it may be unwise for the library to give a green light to plans for a major undertaking. In the long run, the special event may contribute far less to the library's good public relations than lesser assignments faithfully executed.

If the library does not have a Friends group, the author does not recommend that one be organized to wage a campaign or handle a crisis situation. A task force, recruited specifically for the purpose and gracefully dismissed when the battle is over, has proved in her experience to be a far more valuable adjunct than a Friends group whose purpose, once the crisis has subsided, is uncertain and ill-defined. A standing army has a way of becoming an embarrassment. Directors and trustees should not be hasty to organize Friends groups or to encourage citizens to form such groups. The amount of time and effort which must be invested in intelligently directing the activities of the Friends should be carefully weighed against the amount of good they are likely to accomplish. Unless the scales tip heavily in the direction of an organized Friends group, the library would be well advised to explore other, more productive, ways of winning an even wider circle of friends.

11

PRECEPT AND PRACTICE

The opening chapter of this book speaks of
public relations as a way of life, permeating
every facet of the library's operations and
relating to all policies and procedures. In
the intervening chapters, through examples
of precepts put into practice, the author has
endeavored to illustrate what is meant by
good public relations. Good public relations
requires a sensitivity upon the part of the
trustees, the director, and the staff to the
atmosphere of their library; a quick responsiveness to emerging patron needs; a flexible
approach to solving problems; and an enthusiastic acceptance of challenges. Unless
there is a commitment to this concept of
public relations, a steady upbuilding of the
library from such a foundation, all of the
suggested activities will lack unity of pur-

pose and will result in mere motion, instead of coordinated movement toward meaningful goals.

The shortest possible definition of public relations, as detailed in this book, is "creative problem solving." This attitude of mind, which may come slowly at first, will ultimately result in such an innovative approach to the functions of a library that those concerned with its operations will seek out, rather than retreat from, new ways of doing things.

No library can accomplish all of the desired changes — physical or psychological — in a single bound. At first, there must be satisfaction in small beginnings. Everyone knows that the longest journey begins with walking out of the front door. Perhaps that is where the library director and his trustees should begin — by walking out the front door and up the street. Then, they should turn around and return to the library as if they had never been there before. What do they see? What do they sense?

They can make a list of desired physical changes. Less clutter behind the circulation desk. Better lighting. Polishing of light switches and kick-plates on the doors. Replacement of that half-dead ivy in the planters. (Sudden thought: good job for the Garden Club.) This approach will gather momentum. It may finally result in the realization that the library needs a major renovation or an entirely new building.

Perhaps the library administration should do a little role playing and pose a few questions: If I were a skilled technician in an aircraft plant whose job was being phased out, what good would this library be to me? If I were handicapped, partially sighted, spoke poor English, what good would this library be to me? If I were a businessman wanting to trace the development of a product from its invention through its appearance on the market, who would show me how to go about my reference work? It might be a good idea to close the library for a day and try out some group dynamics with staff members under the leadership of a nonlibrary moderator. Let the staff air a few frustrations. Solicit some suggestions for relieving or eliminating them. (An example: must the telephone have such a shrill bell?) Look at the staff handbook. Does it set the right tone for the newcomer or does it read like the Articles of War?

Examine the library's promotional efforts. Have they become routine, uninspired, unimaginative? Is the library passing up good publicity because there's no one to write the news story? Has the library a readily identifiable symbol that appears on books, magazines, records, trailers for films, the side of the bookmobile, the library's letterhead? (Industries spend hundreds of thousands of dollars publicizing their corporate symbols.) In one community, it was discovered, parents didn't even know their children's books were from the public library. They thought the public schools supplied them.

Review the library's rules and regulations. Decide whether they are for the library's benefit or for the patrons'. Justify the library's hours in terms of the living, working, commuting pattern of the community. Think about the composition of the community and then reexamine the book acquisition policies. Does the library purchase the *Evergreen Review* to demonstrate its freedom from fear of censorship or to fulfill legitimate patron requests? What percentage of the families in the community are regular library patrons? Is the figure going up or down? Does the library know why?

Pursuing this course of self-examination, the trustees and the director will soon be able to formulate a plan for the library with long-term goals and short-term benchmarks. A cleaner, better illuminated library with a buzzer instead of a bell on the telephone should be an easily attained short-term goal. A larger paperback collection may not be too difficult to achieve; determining where to shelve it may be a little more perplexing. Rearranging the hours of service may be a great deal more difficult because many libraries have fallen into the trap of hiring people who moonlight at the library (and thus accept lower wages). If a shift in library hours interferes with an employee's primary job, he will first complain and then quit. The library administration has a greater responsibility to serve the public who support it with their taxes than to accommodate the individual staff member who may suffer personal inconvenience if the library's hours are changed. It may require some moral courage to take such a stand.

A better collection, a wider base of patrons, automated

circulation control, a new building, a branch, higher salary scales to attract qualified personnel, paid professionals in all of the appropriate job slots — any or all of these may be the long-term goals of the library. The trustees and the director must identify the desired goals, set up an order of priorities, and begin the strategic moves which will advance the library toward these goals. As the library ingratiates itself with the community through better public relations, its goals will become their goals.

Along the way the trustees and director may receive inspiration or guidance from the manner in which others have met similar problems or reached similar goals. That is the purpose of this book — to stir the minds of library people to a change of base from which they may advance to new and creative ways of solving their problems.

When the author was teaching public relations in library school, she requested her students to identify a problem in a library where they worked or were patrons and to propose a solution. If both the problem and its solution (to be submitted in advance) were acceptable, the term paper for the course would consist of the student's explanation of how to get from the problem to the solution. A wide variety of term paper topics was submitted, including one which reported that the student was a librarian in a metropolitan public school in a run-down neighborhood. The library was located at the rear of a classroom vacated for two periods a day by the class normally using the room. The student's problem, as she saw it, was how to get the teacher to leave the room in more orderly condition.

Asking her to remain after class, the author pointed out that the real problem was to get the library out of the classroom entirely and that anything short of that was no solution at all. The student patiently explained that the school was in a neglected area, that the principal was occupied with other problems, and that she saw no way out of this intolerable situation. The only reply she received was. "Think big. Dream up a solution."

When the term papers were handed in, the student wrote that in thinking over the problem she realized that the city owned portable classrooms and that one could be installed on the unused playground area adjacent to the school. The class

using the "library," which was composed of emotionally disturbed youngsters (it was no wonder that the room was a mess
and the regular teacher resentful at having to vacate it), could
be transferred to the new classroom. This would remove the disturbed children from the main portion of the school, where they
were disruptive, and yet enable them to continue to use the
other facilities such as the gymnasium and the cafeteria.

The classroom thus vacated could be easily converted
to a full-time library. The student even included a drawing indi-
cating where shelves, tables, and chairs could be located. Inviting her to remain after class once more, the instructor said, "This
is an excellent plan. You must ask the principal if it can be carried out." The student, radiant with pleasure, said, "I already
have and they're going to do it."

The student and the instructor agreed that when the
new library was ready to open, the PTA should be invited to use
the quarters for a special social event at which the importance of
the library in the life of elementary school children could be explained to their parents. As the student turned to leave, the instructor reminded her of one final step: "At the library opening,
be sure to compliment the principal on having had such a wonderful idea." The student paused briefly, gave her teacher a knowing nod, and departed. She had learned the ultimate lesson in
public relations.

BIBLIOGRAPHY

Bernays, Edward L. *Public Relations.* University of Oklahoma Press, 1970.

Bundy, Mary Lee and Goodstein, Sylvia, eds. *The Library's Public Revisited.* School of Library and Information Services, University of Maryland, 1967.

Coplan, Kate and Castagna, Edwin, eds. *The Library Reaches Out.* Oceana, 1965.

Garvey, Mona. *Library Displays: Their Purpose, Construction and Use.* H. W. Wilson, 1969.

Golden, Hal and Hanson, Kitty, *How to Plan, Produce and Publicize Special Events.* Oceana, 1960.

Loizeaux, Marie D. *Publicity Primer.* 4th ed., 2d ptg. H. W. Wilson, 1967.

Norton, Alice, *Public Relations: Information Sources.* (Management Information Guide Series) Gale, 1970 [1971].

Wallace, Sarah L. ed. *Friends of the Library. Organization and Activities.* American Library Association, 1962.

Wallace, Sarah L. *Patrons Are People: How to Be a Model Librarian.* 2d (rev.) ed. American Library Association, 1956.

Young, Virginia G., ed. *The Library Trustee: A Practical Guidebook.* 2d ed. Bowker, 1969.

INDEX